Elephant Cake Walk

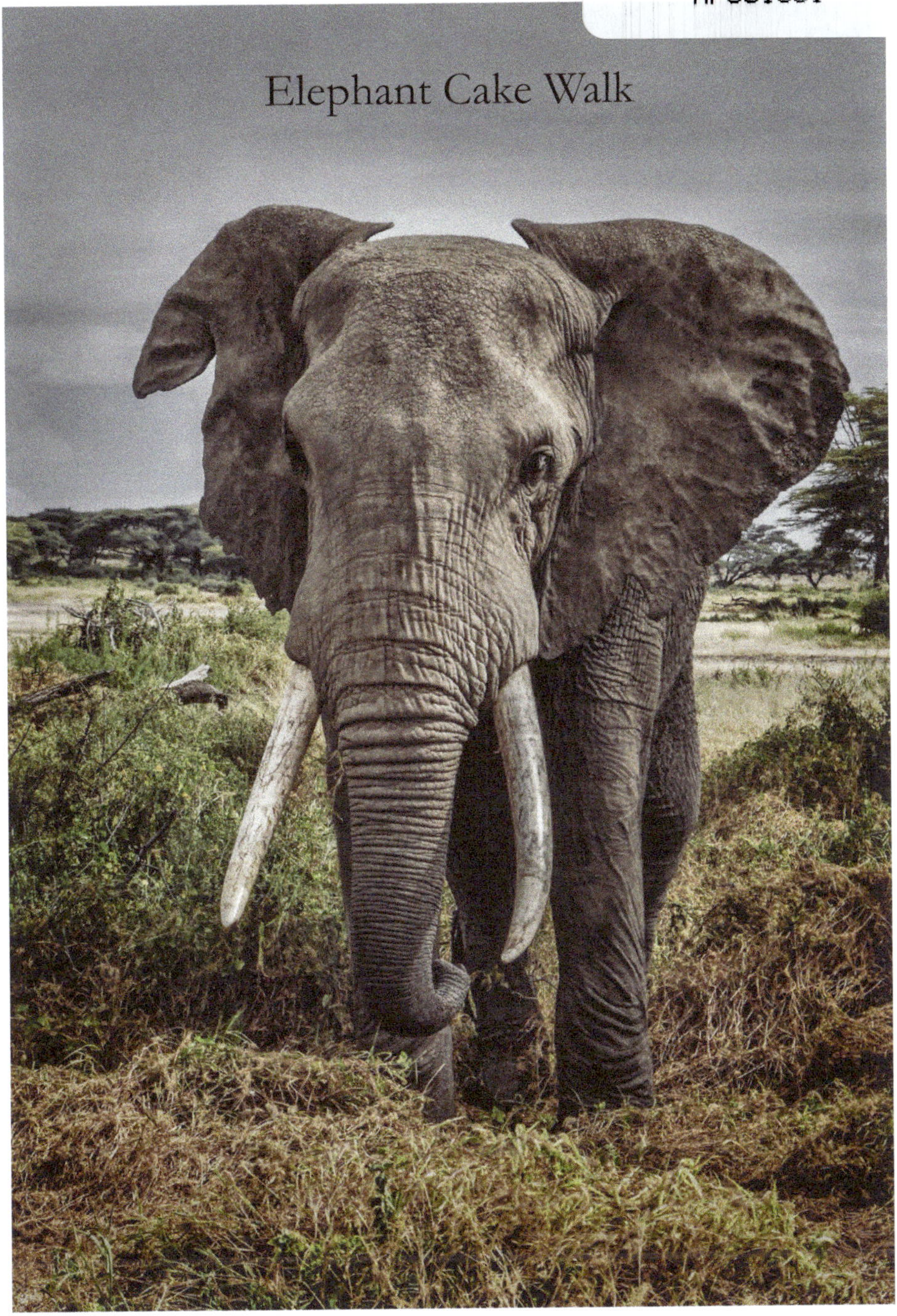

Elephant Photo by Carol Leadbetter

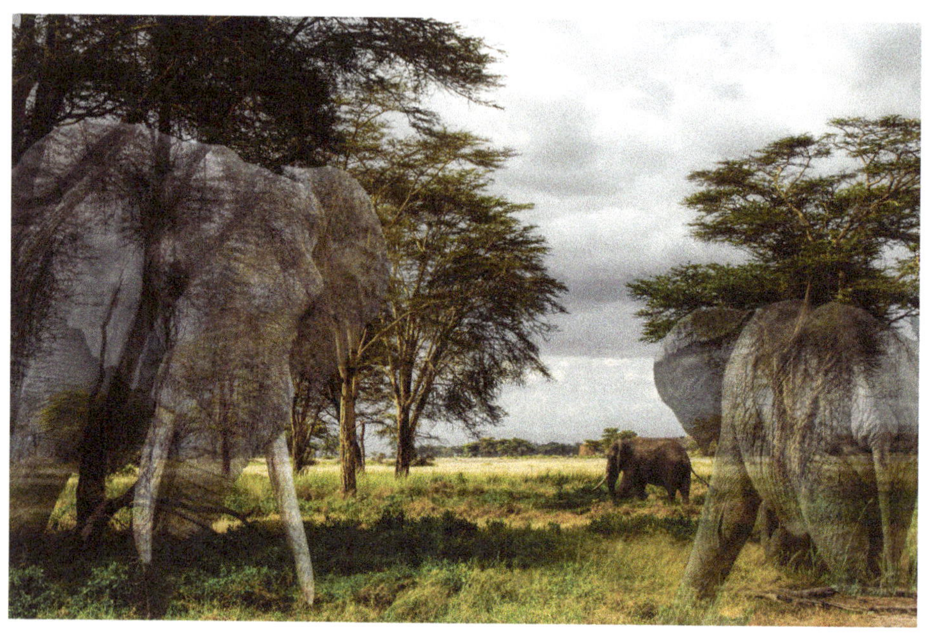

Elephants fading Photo by Carol Leadbetter

Elephant Cake Walk

Andrew H. Oerke

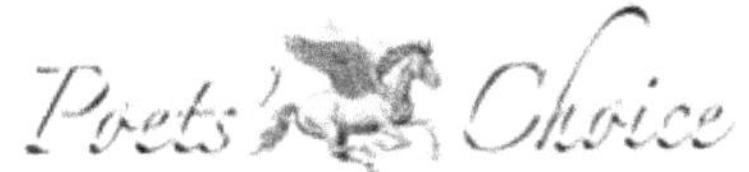

Poets' Choice Publishing

Printed in the United States of America

Cover Photo: "Amboseli Dawn" by Cynthia Moss,
Amboseli Elephant Trust
Author's photo: Dr. Ryan Jackson, MD

Consultant work:
www.WilliamMeredithFoundation.org

Bulk discounts available through www.Poets-Choice.com

Library of Congress Cataloging-in-Publication Data pending
ISBN 978-0-9972629-7-1

Poets' Choice

Poets' Choice Publishing
337 Kitemaug Road
Uncasville, CT 06382
Poets-Choice.com

To my beloved Anitra

with whom I saw the earth
and its creatures with new eyes
in our adventure of learning to heal the earth

Acknowledgements

Clark Street Review ("Old Fez"), *Languageandculture.net* ("Upside-down Tree #2," "TB Ward"), *New Yorker* ("In the Village"), *Nomad's Choir* ("Tommies"), *Poetalk* ("Night Train to Kisumu,"), *Poet's Art* ("Lioness Dining"), *Poet's Pen* ("Gorilla in Glass," "Nefertiti, Berlin-Dahlem"), *Portals* ("The Barrage"), *River Oak Review* ("The Nightfishers of Dakar"), *Write On!* ("The Totems of the Hotel Ivoire") Some poems have been slightly revised.

The following poems were previously printed in Andrew Oerke's *African Stiltdancer* and are reprinted by permission of Swan Books: "In the Village," "The Hippo's Head," "Black Christ," "'Upside-down Tree,' the Baobab," "Night Train to Kisumu," "Lamu," "The Blowfish," Old Fez," "Impalas" [from "A Small Bestiary from the Grasslands"], "Refugees," "Nile Crocodile," "TB Ward," "The Barrage," "Addis at Easter," "Mount Malawi," "Dawn in the Highlands" [formerly "Zomba Plateau"], and "Nomads." The following poems were previously printed in Andrew Oerke's *San Miguel de Allende* and are reprinted by permission of Swan Books: "The Sun," and "Return from the Sun." The following poems were previously printed in Andrew Oerke's *Never Seek to Tell Thy Love* and are reprinted by permission of GCEEF Publishers: "Amenhotep III and Queen Tiye, Cairo Museum," and "Nefertiti, Berlin-Dahlem." Some poems have been slightly revised.

Thanks to Cynthia Moss, Founding Director of the Amboseli Elephant Trust for photographs of Amboseli elephants and other animals embedded within the poems. Thanks to the Amboseli Trust for permissions. Also thanks to Mike Dexter, Botswana.

Thanks to Kathleen Coffee, who assembled and edited unpublished and published poems. Thanks to the creative editorship of Richard Harteis, whose dedication to the Meredith Foundation and Poet's Choice Press made this volume possible. Thanks for the construction of the volume by Barbara Shaw. Thanks to Kirsten, Jarad, and Greta who as children in a strange land showed me what excitement the creatures of this land stirred in their hearts. And to Cashen and Odin, whose wonderment recalled decades of African adventures.

PRAISE FOR PREVIOUS BOOKS BY ANDREW OERKE

San Miguel de Allende (2005)

"Andrew Oerke's poetry is original, vivid and eloquent. I reread his work with great pleasure and enlightenment.

—Harold Bloom

"Andrew Oerke writes with extraordinary depth of feeling and mastery of form. His poems are an American treasure."

—Jewel Spears Brooker

"Andrew Oerke constantly surprises with unexpected images and turns of phrase. He moves comfortably between the colloquial and the poetic."

—Herbert Lindenberger, Avalon Professor of Humanities, Stanford University.

African Stiltdancer (2006)

"Andrew Oerke's work is a window on the world, a world seen through the compassionate eyes of a fellow pilgrim. In the exquisite particulars of Africa, he sings the human condition, 'in the heart's duress, on the heart's behalf.' He is a marvel, moving from one stunning image to the next with the ease of a chameleon moving from fire to water."

—Richard Harteis and William Meredith

Never Seek to Tell Thy Love (2010)

"Andrew Oerke has wandered over the entire globe. His eye is shrewd, his mind capacious, and his generosity toward humankind is endless. His poems, whether set in Africa, Mexico, or in the United States, invariably offer fresh perspectives upon the reality he has encountered.

I particularly am moved by his Mexican sequence, where an elegiac intensity permeates his work. Though his subjectivity is admirably realized, he refreshes the reader with an achieved singularity. His is a singularity that cares both for itself and for others, unlike certain other poets who attain their individualities by being indifferent both to the self and to others.

Oerke's voice has matured into one that is very much his own. He has absorbed and transformed the influence of his former teacher, the admirable American poet Mark Strand. When I consider that Oerke is very much a person who lives out in the world, actively restoring the ecological balance of the oceans, and aiding other men and women to live better lives, I am profoundly moved that he should also have his sustained ability to enter, again and again, the universe of reverie and of quiet contemplation."

—Harold Bloom, Stirling Professor of the Humanities at Yale University. Comments on the occasion of the bestowal of the Award for Literature to Andrew Oerke by the United Nations Society of Writers and Artists at the UN.

The Wall (2015)

"Andrew Oerke is fearless. Who else could possibly write 19 poems (of 43) featuring walls—each more imaginative than the last. Some poems are exaltations, some moral occasions, others witty and playful; and, in all, the poetic sense comes through Oerke's self honesty. He's skilled in story compression and solves interesting linguistic problems in the process. Most of all, this is relevant work that will surely strike a major note with readers."

—Grace Cavalieri, Producer/Host, "The Poet and the Poem from the Library of Congress"

CONTENTS

IV. African Haiku

V. The Game Park

VI. Subsaharan Adventures

I

African Dawns

In the Beginning: Genus & Species,
Talk & Scribble, Civilization & Soul,
What's Next?

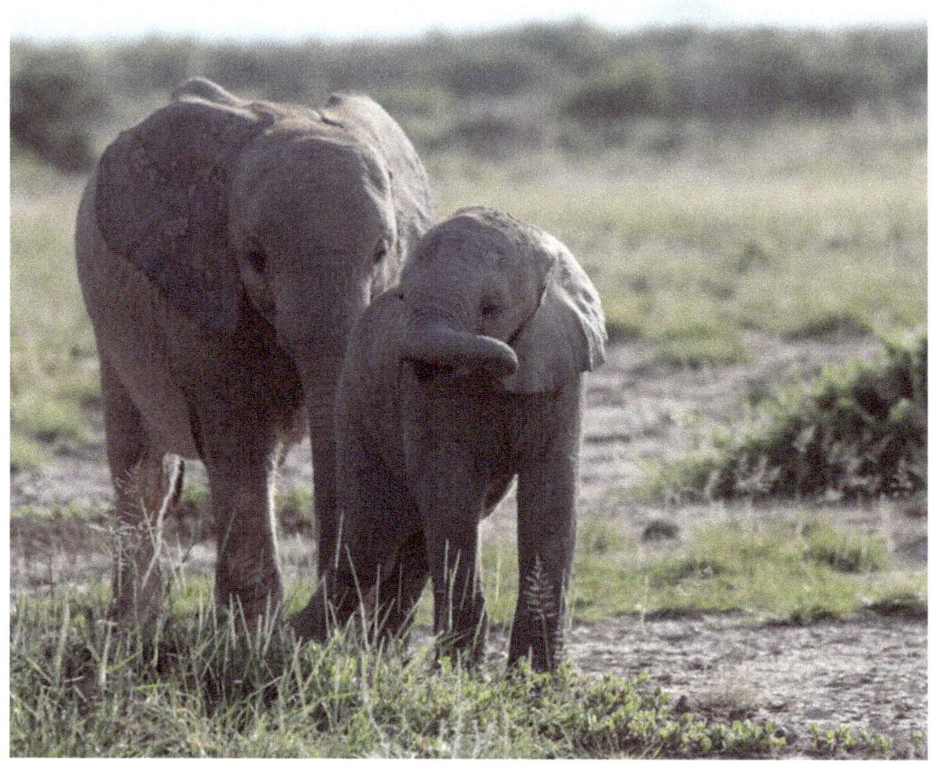

Elephant Cake Walk Photo by Cynthia Moss, Ambosei Elephant Trust

ELEPHANT CAKE WALK, Botswana

I was someone outside himself spying through a
blind on a French-fried waterhole in Botswana:
Lightning in the window flashes me back to then,
and I'm there again the day the Dry Season
converted to Yoga, stood on its head
but with Christian agapé baptized some nearly dead
elephants in the Okavango Delta:
Now the waterhole's dustbowl is bathtub gin
drunken beasts gulp n gallop around in.

It was total immersion in raindrop redemption
when a monsoon from over the sea washed us
in the white lightning blood of its storm n drench.

Clouds were too full of themselves to be
what clouds are. Surface tension, skinned by windshear,
dropped its H_2O on a wasteland so sere,
and its crust so baked, it couldn't stop
snap-crackle-n-popping like mummy wrap.

Pachyderms wankled rotary pistons
churning away to happy-go-lucky heartbeats.
Graf Zeppelins on like tree stumps hoofed a ballet
to behold! Gravity raised its eyebrows, but
how to vault as high as tuskers can strut?
We cheer the bull's lungs whose trumpet-hot trunk
rattled the Sky's bones with a Mardi Gras din
and we'll kick a good cake walk when the saints march in.

Night's ink spots Rorschach my pages, and though
gizmos bugle my brains out on googly stages,
my ballpoint's old baton sways with Sammy Kaye;
my graphite horn sobs with mournful Miles.
I tinpan gravel's gold in the voice box of Louis the A.

TALK, SCRIBBLE & SOUL, the Super Three

Talk, Scribble & Soul were born in Africa.
What will pop out of Africa next, I wonder.
Who'd've thought the virtual'd be the New World Order?
That in the beginning was symbolic logic
deconstructed by Shakespeare to comic n tragic?

Maybe words were a gift from the Sun God,
for if out star hadn't downsized, it couldn't
have called itself up in our eyes. Let's hope
the I-Told-You-So Past won't sucker us into
spiral-ringed galactic Cirque du Soleil's
tombstones that can still make eyesight insight's pupil.

In Hubble's keg, other suns bubble n wink.
Planets don't blink though the earth can think,
and our alphabet brew toasts words that can do
for words without deeds do not to heaven go.

Talk, Scribble & Soul, the jellyroll 3, strutted
their big stuff on the long march out of Africa.
Listen up; don't shut up; do-be do-be do.
Throttle all out like jazz and scat free, or
worship Hollywood stars, hold tardy views,
and "serve ye this day the devil you choose."
If you got the money, Honey, let's make some news.

THE WITCHDOCTOR'S DANCE, Southern Africa

His shadow's a cutout cut out of darker looks.
It jumps out of black like a Jack-in-the-Box.
He's a dust devil in a sinister uproar;
a sight for sore eyes in his furore.
He's a stork stifflegging "The Leopardskin Rag."
He's Death dressed up like a gunny-sack hag.

Powder of moon dust and the cauldron crackles:
Chromosomes bolt out of their starting blocks
and pass batons on on the run gen to gen
on the upward trail of Here We Come Again,
a little bit changed from the ones we have been.

It started when the witchdoctor rolled the bones
and his spooky mouth spoke a world into being.
Now, we shoot starfish in Hubble's barrel, don't we?
We wormhole back to the First Concentration,
which divested or we couldn't have invested.
Let's hope his bewitching dance remains intact
and Moby's not Ahabbed with harpoons of fact,
for his drumming feet invented a world.

From androgynous froth a child went forth to
a land of graveyards & names. 20-carat nouns
swore they'd be true. Verbs said, "Though we're here,
we can hitch a ride with them to Back Then
since Now is two-faced, hermaphroditically
Mars & Venus, a Past or Future When."

That's how an empty mouth blew out the old world,
and words flew through the air with the greatest of ease
like the "daring young man on the flying trapeze."

From Lake Nakaru's reeds to Mombasa's shores
Kool-Aid flamingos work their wrong way-hinged
crutches on wings to spy on the dark side and
in their carotenoid camouflage they
are indistinguishable from the twilight.
—Two rhyming end lines on the last flight tonight.

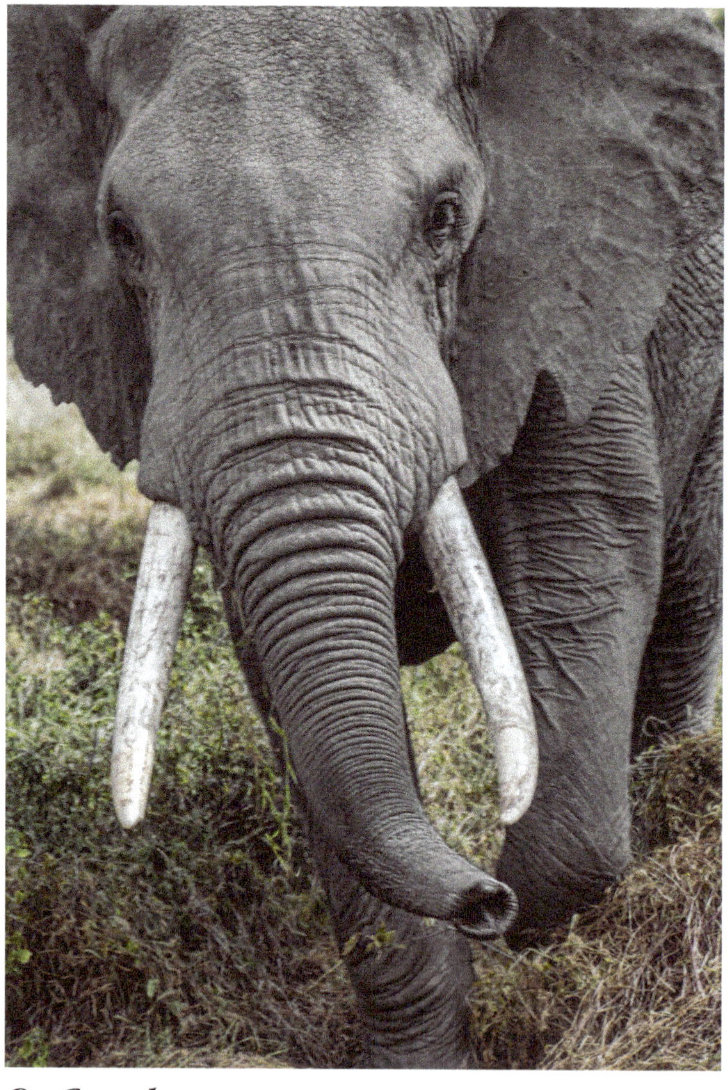

On Guard Photo by Carol Leadbetter

SECOND AFRICAN STILTDANCER

Each leg swinging like a scythe, he harvests our eyes.
He casts firelight's phantasmagorical spell
on a Saturday night in the ninth rung of hell.

His matador cape veronicas the smoke
bull-rushing from the chute of his shadow
that's tailored to suit him, tags him like Fido.
The smoke thins like yesterday's intentions
whose resolutions never meant to be go-go,
or understand that Donne's bell rings for thee.

The Stiltdancer's an "objective correlative" for
a printer's devil's inklings stretching for more.
But how to grasp the gist of this guy's jive?
He rolls the bones of survival for a whole tribe.

On seven-league boots the dancer repeats
his shadow's shuck. He kicks flames with chopstick feet.
We jump for joy for Fear's a cherished delight,
blueprint n charter for hide-n-seek games
and Hollywood's chase-n-escapecapade scenes.
Of this much we're certain; this much we know.
The rest is up to you so far as it goes though.

THIRD AFRICAN STILTDANCER

The Stiltdancer's shadows magic-lantern the walls.
He's Dark Night dressed in Carnate Corpus Taboo.
Would we stood taller when we light up our lives
with slugs of lead trailing footprints of black blood.

The Dancer's cape is cut from midnight's cloth.
His cloak's a shadow escaping Plato's cave.
His shadow's a clutter of bats whose stiff elbows
are old typewriter keys chattering poems onto paper.

In Plato's grotto, the flames rise n fall
but the greatest eminence of them all's the ghost
in the machine of Language, whose dancing pegs
waltz on stages called bookshelves talking big
beyond the baby steps actually taken.

Sticky sounds in grammatical tethers and their
alphabetic slaves tell the old old story of
"Endless Desire versus Impossible Love."

Lips livid as bruises, eyes blinking like stars,
he skips on league-long boots past our laissez-faire
Book of Days. We scatter like waterfowl
when Dingo Dog rushes for the waterhole.
We scream, for fear's a dark n devilish delight:
Go to the flicks, better kick for cover;
it's one damn chase n escape scene after another.

THE SUN KINGDOM IN ABU SIMBEL

Our brain cells invented baked clay tablets
that left clues for the Gray Lady's science pundits,
and who is to say this is not the case?
(Pages n pages of lemon-ink illustrations.)

When sounds shuttle back n forth between larynx
n tympanum, they can say "sun" so much the source
gets more real than it was, times, of course,
as many times as the word-bird flew from our mouths
like moths to the light, light being what life's all about.

Our planet Wurlitzer's a blue-marbled mirror
so the Aten can anchor himself in our eyes
with words whose weight's not swept by the tides.
Poetry is Apollo's fortune-cookie prize
cooked up by a ratty chef in the basement.

The Twilight Zone says: Peripheral vision sees best
that cliffs are where wings can niche a safe nest.
Be bimodal as crepuscule, whose shadows blender
light with dark, like Orson's Magnificent Ampersands
who walk n talk with us hand in hand. Every
18 and a half years Sun & Moon make love
on the altar of Abu Symbol, colossal blind relic now
where the "lone and level sands stretch far away."

AFRICAN NIGHTS

When African nights are read, it's by Braille.
In this planetarium's plasma-punctured visual
it's so milky you can't find the installations
up there called the godly constellations.

You grope your way towards the rest house whose
kerosene lantern can't fuse its wick.
Night's calamitous creatures love the weakest ruse.
Like the Zen Master called Life, they brook no excuse.

Hyenas and a cobra's 40-foot hissy-fit
will kill Bill kindly, not slowly with a kiss.
So our hands taught our minds to think sharp,
to blunt our clubs but whittle a fine-point edge.
That's how the Tool Age staked out livelihood's footage
and conquered the world "for better or worse," says the sage.

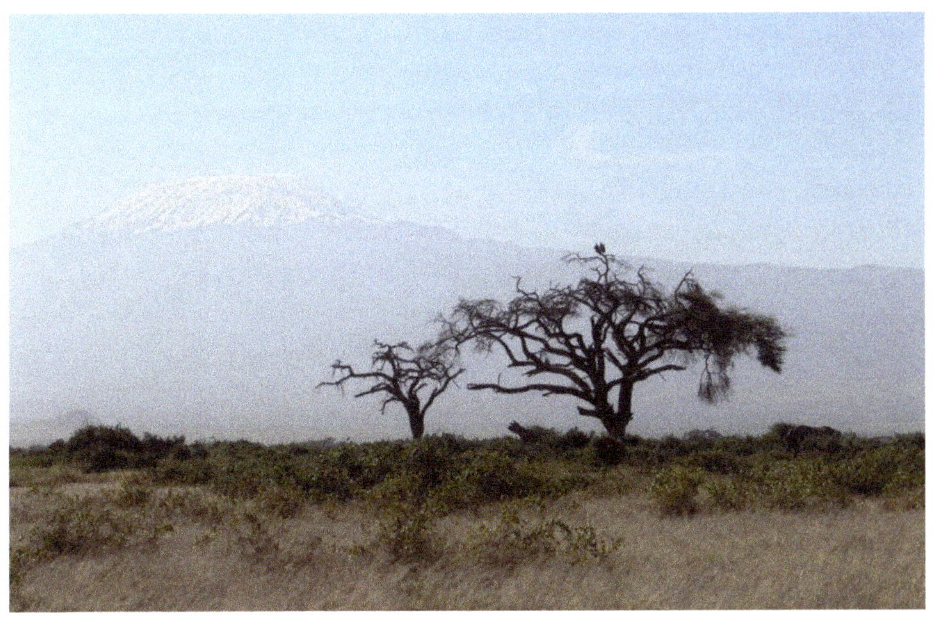

Amboseli Dawn Photo by Cynthia Moss, Amboseli Elephant Trust

AMBOSELI DAWN

The Sun shatters the lance shafts of the Armies of the Night
though the sheen of their spears was like stars on the sea
when the blue wave rolls nightly on deep Galilee.

Now the rising sun's isinglass furnace issues smoke.
Night's mantle reverses to its inner lining blue cape.
In the still-brisk air, winds blow browsers & grazers
like cloud-drifting herds across their dawn-n-dew-freshened food.
The sun's dandelion-like mane may shield them
from poachers camouflaged in midnight's reticulated fatigues.

As light struggles out of its chamber of nightmares
it releases our ancestors' indentured souls
from their fireflies, Coleman lanterns, and twinkling stars
but not from the bicycle-reflector eyes of the creepy hyenas
whose Chucky-like, devilish-smart eyes thrive on death as we all do.

Our ancestors emerge like negatives exposed in
a darkroom of nitrate solutions. They dog our day,
but have neither shadow nor substance. We are they.

II

Animals in the High Plains

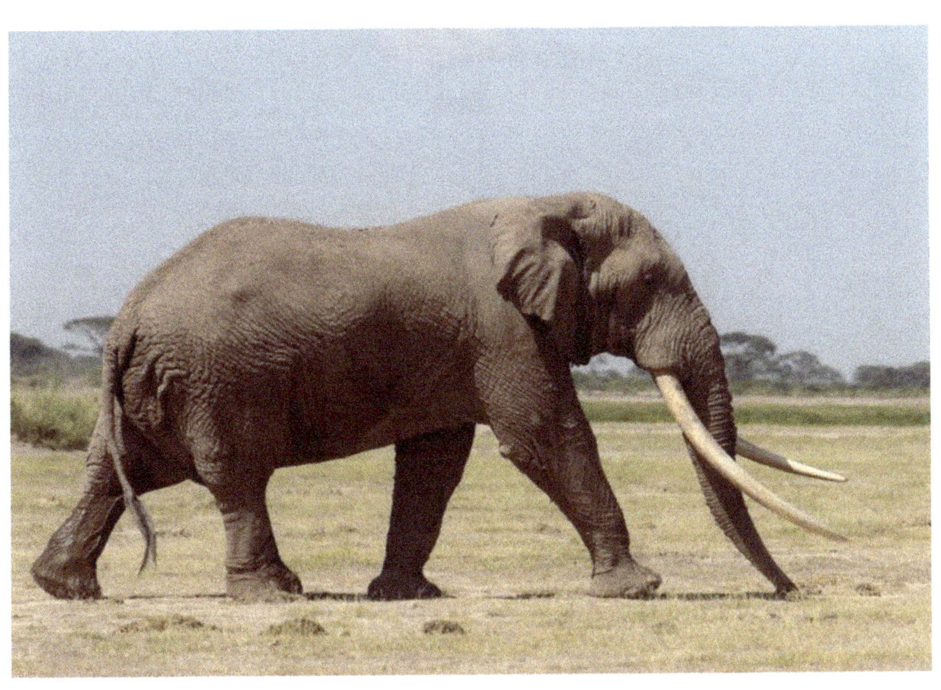

Photo by Cynthia Moss,Amboseli Elephant Trust

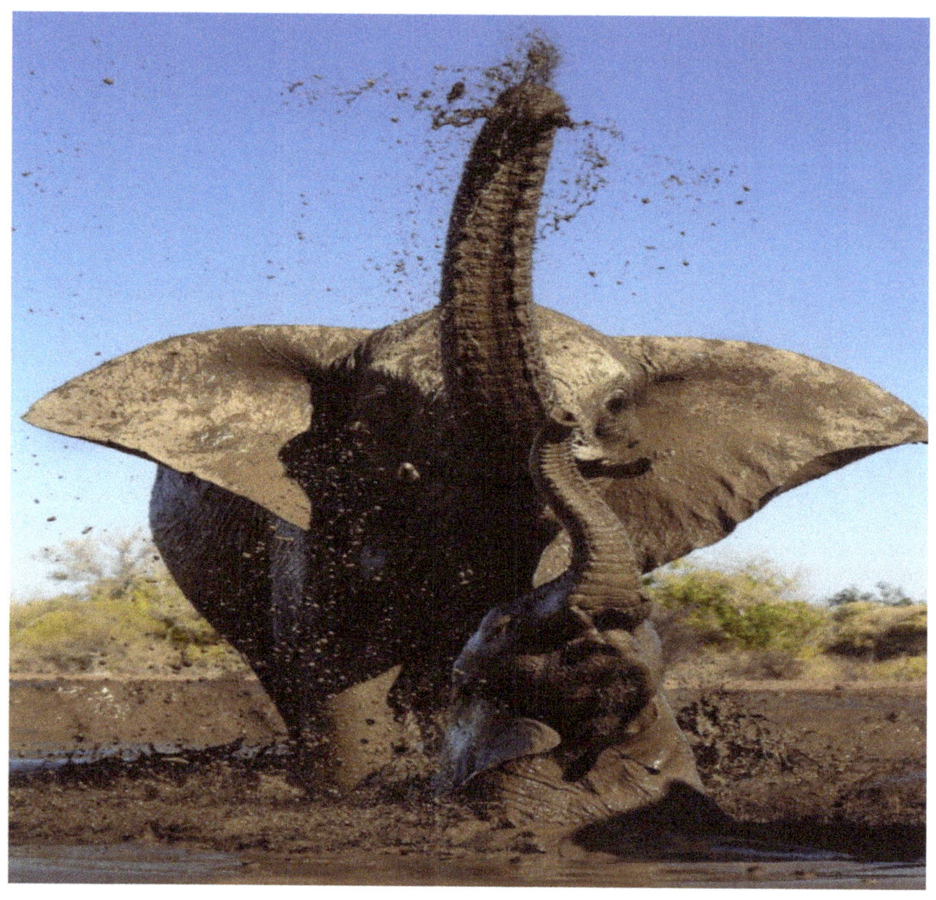

Jubilation Cake Walk Photo by Mike Dexter

JUBILATION CAKE WALK

Rain tapping the windowpane types out an old-time version
remembered by heart in which a baptism totally immerses
a death march of long noses. Trumpeting redemption's reprieve
they trot a conga line that jubilation weaves;
they bounce a bongo dance of deliverance,
rinsing off the dirt with not one penny for penance.

Leaves hang like hounds' ears under a soggy weight.
Clouds had swollen to so full of themselves they cast out
what they were. They emptied their lighter-than-air water bags
which is all that mattered. They joined forces with whatever
soil can be, from which we bloomed later than when gametes mated.

Lightning precipitates a downpour out of saturated fog
invigorating rhizomes jabbing deep in the swale
where tendrils' fingertips read fortune cookies by Braille.
The hose-noses' futures are no longer up for grabs.
They gyrate their ponderous hydro-pod pads,
syncopating their rhythms to the heartbeats in our own bods
in the wake of a kind of relief so unbearably
weightless it raises Gravity's limbo-bar.
We didn't know how to strut as high as their hips can flare
but recognize the cake-walk that kips our hopes up there, too.
Rather a rainy-day gospel than the dust bowl blues.

As darkness showers letters on my pages
I start to swing. I shuffle and sway.
My horny pen is my trumpet; I blow my brains out
like Miles Davis and Louis the A.

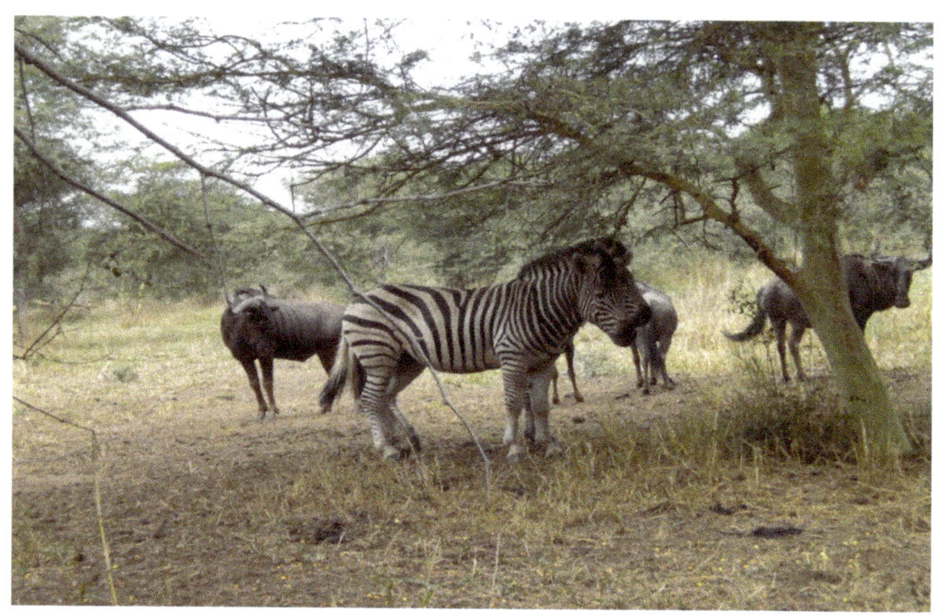

Wildebeest with Zebras Photo by Lance Cole

WILDEBEEST

A beige fringe hangs from his hazelnut neck,
and a stringy goatee dangles from his chin
all the way down to his milk-chocolate chest.
Suddenly his puny horns crack a sidelong buck
and jerk as he kicks up a funky spasm
and then casually returns to his grazing.
This collection of spare parts from a junk yard
was put together hastily but successfully
judging from the millions massing for migration
on the Serengeti's unenveloped plain.

This unlikely stiff-legged gallop, as if he were
hobbled, shoulders hunched low in anxious motions
of the head eavesdropping on the ground; this fully
suspicious beast, keeps gazing and grazing ahead
to stuff his jaws with grass and straw that will
keep him going, though in his final spasm
of old age and weakness he still kicks and screams
to dodge the casket of Leo's greedy throat
where Wildie's ancient beard of wisdom doesn't help
when faced with the question: How many new gnus
does it take to stuff a lion's scruffy old pelt?

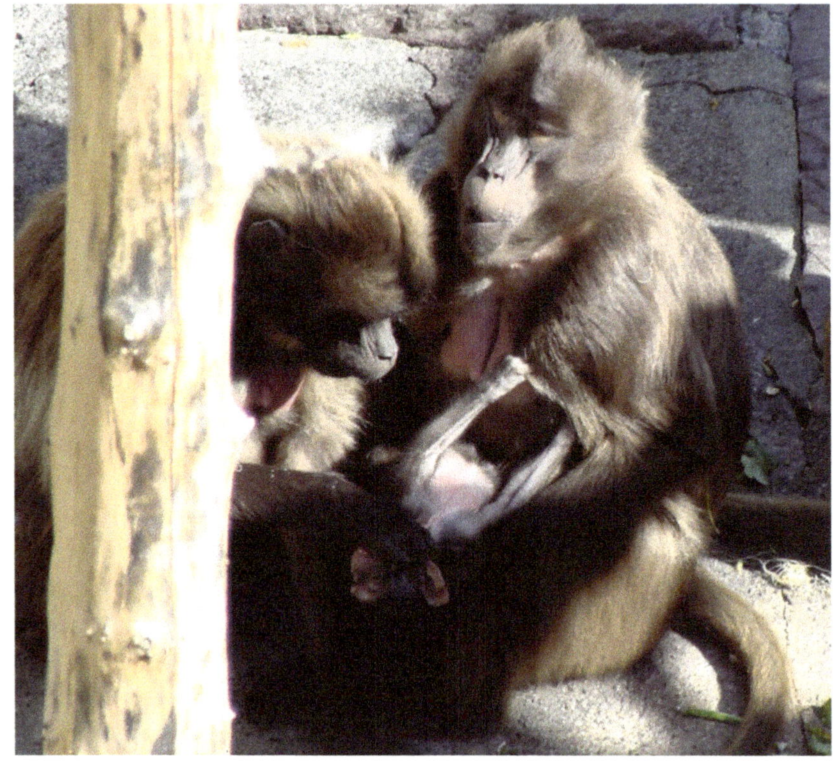

Baboon Photo by A. Thorhaug

BABOON VAVOOM

He rubber-bumpers upndown on my Land Rover bonnet.
He is the fang I looked like back then during
those brinks of survival in the killing fields.
My windscreen swoons through Time's rearview mirror.

He glances at everything except for my eyes.
With peripheral vision he tests me for fight or flight
to see if I flinch. We stall there at the
bellybutton centràl in Africa and I feel my hair stiffen
eeking on end like hackles of fight-to-the-finish fur.
My eyebrows ridge up, scowling fierce as the deepest cave.

How much of me is him; how much of him
is still me? The mirror-images are deaf n dumb.
Suddenly our looks lock in a defiant
exchange of recognition. A spark in each other's eyes
makes four fireflies in sync. Then the flicker falls dead
as a fossil that's been lurking in strata though loses cover
millennia later. He bares his three-penny teeth, taunts me
through the bug-spotted windscreen; and swivels me a mismatch:
my pale face and his spectacular buttocks,
him and his patriotic red n blue rectum-spectrum.

OSTRICH

Its bulbous, ovalesque body lollops in slingshot
strides on skimpy legs with a stretched-erect
rubber-chicken neck. Its squashed beak and pinhead head,
bug-eyed alert, do the funky turkey
tracking on feet that look like a hat rack
that spokes around fast as a roadrunner
that leaves most everything else in the dust.

The bulging drumsticks blur in quick motion
as they batter the sands at 40 mph in
great scrubbing dollops of long looping strides
as the swollen, plumed football-with-legs floats
level, kicking seven-league, dinky dust devils behind it.

Instead of poking its head in the sand
it sidesteps the lion's great grate-like jaws
and the back-hoe hinges of hyenas. But no weather
or leopard will keep him from galumphing to
meet his mate and be a quadruped double bed
rocking like twin feather-dusters in turmoil,
that lay big thick shells tourists get a kick
out of but only their chicks can kick themselves out of.

GIRAFFE

A Wankel-type of piston-and-gear rotation
unseen under his dappled-and-dapper clown suit
levels his shock absorbers at even keel.
And he sails like a yacht; he floats like a kite.
He nibbles the leaf and spits out a thorn.
A butterfly tees up on his knobby horn.
A slurry of cells, he's never in a hurry
unless he's kicking a predator's teeth out, bam!

He's been stretched till he's Anti-gravity
on a bungee cord but only on the upward bounce.
In due time he may make it to the clouds
with a clerical collar's cumulous ruff.
At his dainty four-frames-per-second speed
I'd like to see him trip the light fantastic.
I'd like to see him perform a slow ballet
with Maria Tallchief in a no-ceiling room
with just the walls watching (except for me).
I'd issue blanket amnesty for jailhouse giraffes
behind bars in so-called civilized states.
It's as if he'd stretched his neck out like
a telescope standing on end as he reaches
for one more bite full after another,
his eye in the sky, his hooves on the ground.
When he moves, the camera moves with him.

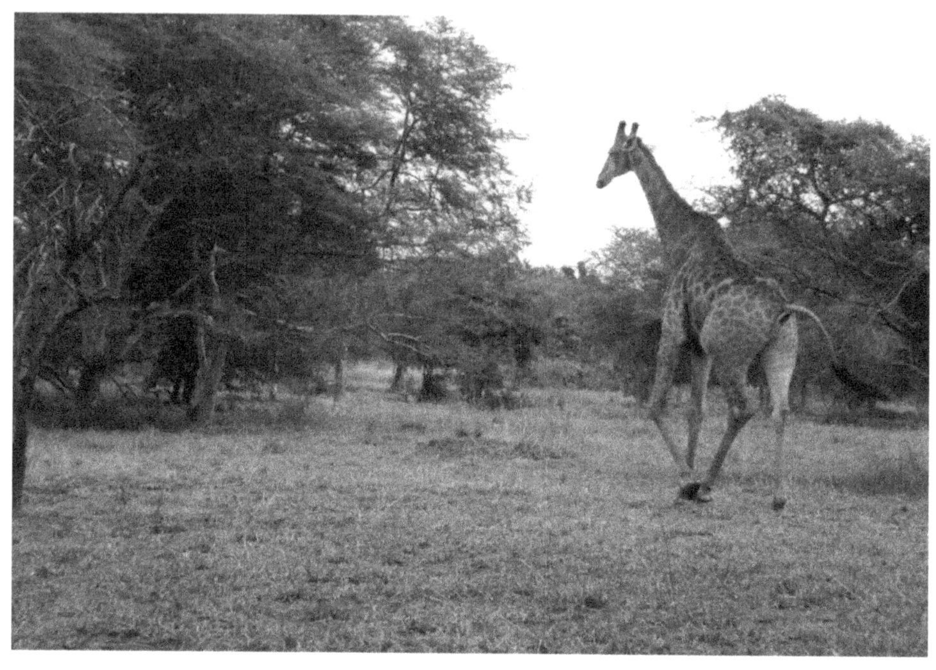

Giraffe Photo by Lance Cole

TOMMIES

It's as if they're dangling from sky hooks
and can slow the clock for a sec at the leap-top
as Nijinsky did in the daguerreotypes.
Their black-and-white stripes are strokes
not to show themselves off but for camouflage;
also to make them look even streakier-faster.
Only their twitchy tails tattle on
their whereabouts when they slowpoke the fields
nimbly as goats. Then at the merest creak
they bobble up and down like ping-pong balls
resolving a survival-of-the-fittest lottery,
or they coil-spring like Gerald McBoing-Boings.
Follow the bouncing ball at the sink of the screen
and sing along with the piston-like tommies.

They populate every East African game park
as if the lead gene out of Noah's ark.
They know the art of escape top to bottom
as if taught by Houdini how to break bonds,
who survived, his limbs tangled up in sailors' knots,
though he couldn't spring like a trampoline-buck,
which is how tommies' escape artistry escapes tough luck.

IMPALAS

Impalas invent a realm
between ascent and descent,
up and down,
and then they're gone
though the image lingers on
as the essence of reminiscence.

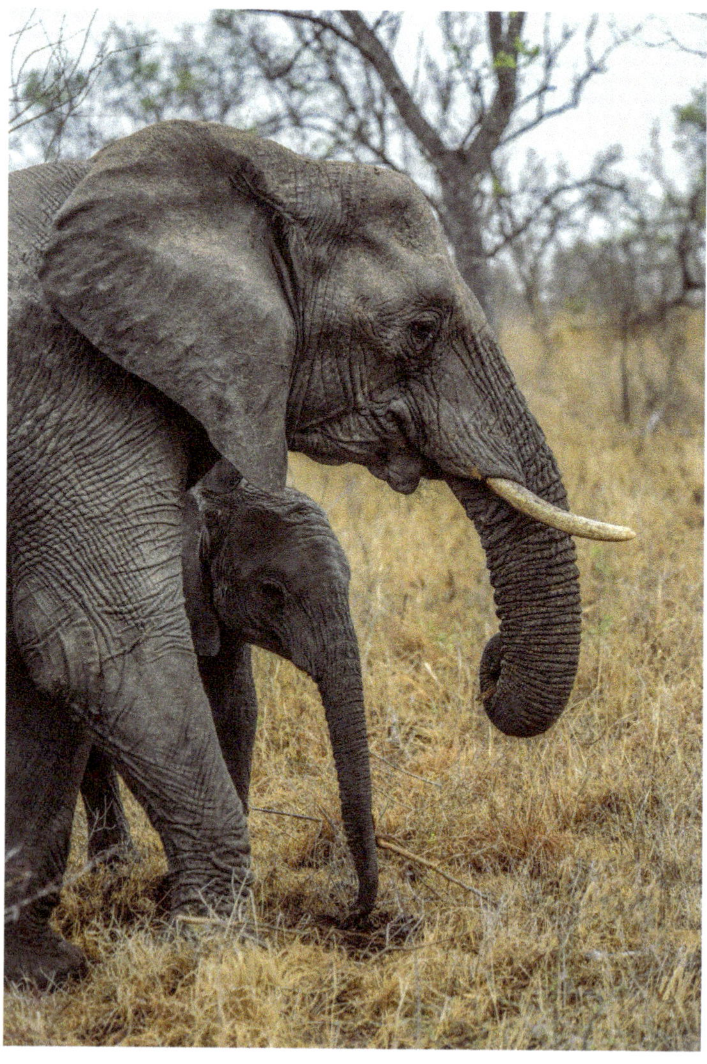

Someone to watch over me Photo by Carol Leadbetter

MALAWI DAWN, for Grets

Fishermen dip slow, dip quick,
flick-flick, as they wade through a
low tide's flat pink sheet of glass.
They groom and glean the jaws of Dawn.
They lure the quicksilver shadows
into the net's invisibly treacherous yawn.

The seconds fall slow as snow,
though it never snows here in Ng'ambo.

It is time for breakfast.
The Sky steps into its light blue skin,
slips into its Lucky Luciano cloud-jacket,
removes the Haviland china from the shelf
and serves cappuccino in porcelain cups
with creamy white-felt gloves.

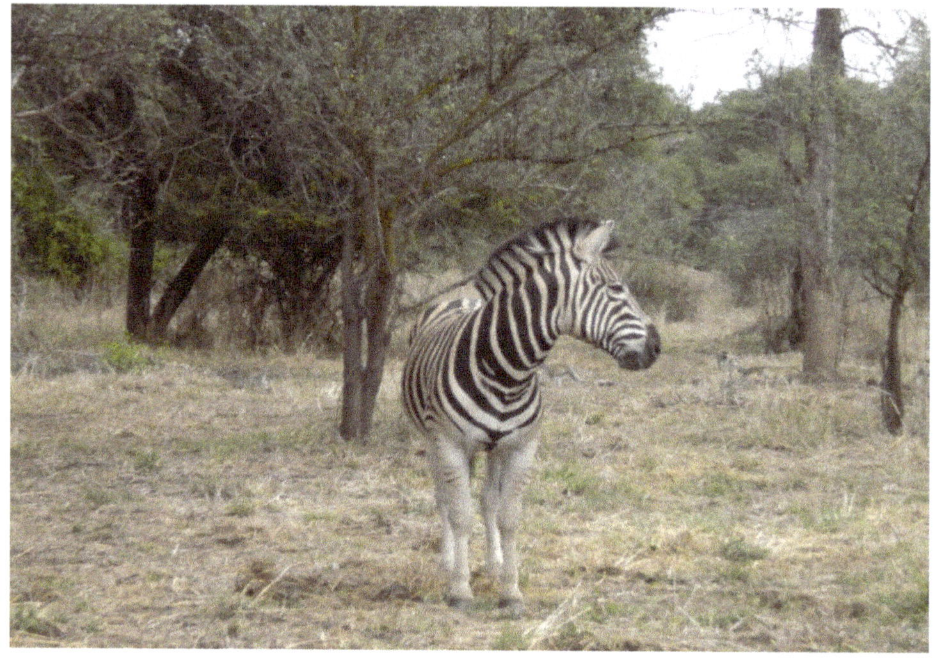

Malawi Dawn Photo by Lance Cole

TANZANIAN PLOVER

The plover dives for the exact same spot
through zillions of bulls eyes stacked in the air
for the arrowhead of her beak to pierce through,
quill after quill. Picture her on target
from three thousand miles away. Over and over
she splits the arrow already in the bulls eye, the nest
from last year, with greater accuracy than Robin Hood
could at short distances. She evades the eagle,
the hawk, and wedges through sky molecules battling
against her progress. She skims in a low arc like a missile,
and everything working according to muscles con-
tracting, relaxing to her systole-diastole heart.
On the treadle of her wings she weaves a cradle
for eggs baked in the oven-down of her breast in her nest.
They will burst into the plumage of her very own
Christ Child, her plover chick, dear to its
mother's high-flying, self-sacrificing breast.

AFRICAN BUTTERFLY

A semaphore of Nature's flags
releases anagrams to
scramble the wind. Wings dive,
splash, ripple apart: Wing-chips
of palette knife, yodeling throat,
stripper socking up and down
Jacob's ladder shimmy and shake.

A kite snaps loose and tent flaps bat
in the breeze. Drift me, pretty paddle
wheel, through currents blue. Balance me
still on the lip of a tin can,
a thought about to speak.
Then scatter me, dandelion seeds,
like flour sifted to a fine forgetting.

Articulate banjo notes rise,
fall, pick the strings of sight,
then settle to startle themselves
with us: Our eyes are such serious scales;
our wings are shrunk to the size
of an ear. Please us with patterns
that do not matter; teach us to love what is sheer.

III

In the Village

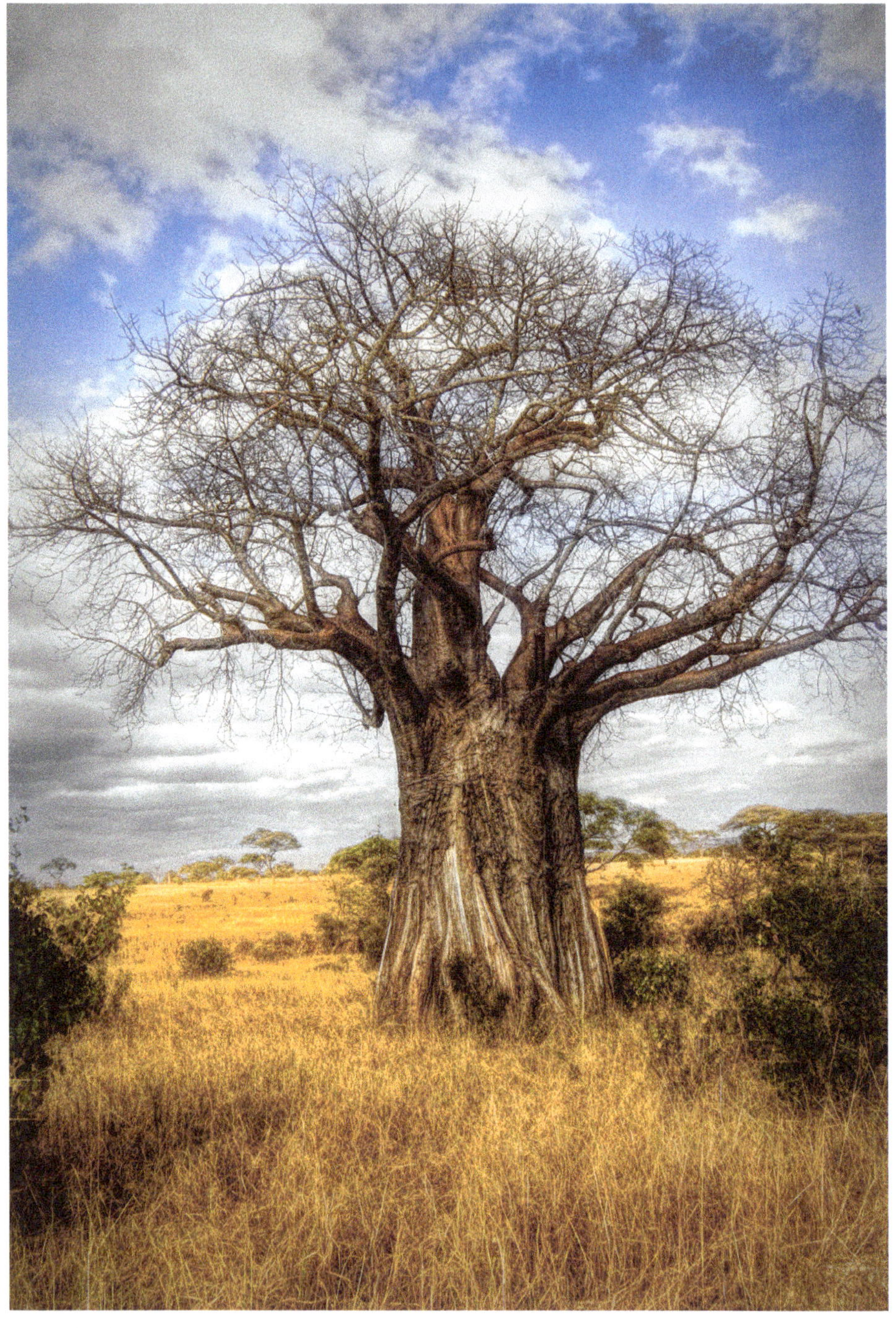

Baobab tree Photo by Carol Leadbetter

BLACK CHRIST

I think that Jesus was black
because I saw him in a niche
in a cathedral, sagging on
a cross, black as Louis Armstrong.
His ebony agony sang
spirituals, the muscles and bones
jutting and jagged in resistance
to the slack solo of his weight;
and all the jazz and racket of death
was in his posture, and all the
stretched-out eloquence of a hurdler.

It was suffering that painted
him black and sculpted the climax
of his final dance. Sprung like a jack,
he hung impaled on the crosshairs
of a sight at the split-second
of impact, with his swarthy face
buckled blindly on one shoulder;
or he seemed to not wish to see
who maimed him, so shuttered his eyes
and listened to the beat in his loins.
His arms stuck out like two trombones.

In back of him fell a red velvet
curtain that was cloyed with tarnished
silver hearts, as though his subjects
were in hock to him, and at his feet
candles guttered in scarlet cups,
the ephemeral jewels of the poor.
I watched the Mississippi night
of his soul, and pondered the jive
of his gospel, till he became
an icon in the cathedral again:
black statue with real hair.

IN THE VILLAGE

In the village in the village in the village
life repeats itself, life repeats itself.
There is sunlight, there is darkness. The dark
repeats itself, the light repeats itself.
Yet life is never dull. It pats the drum hide
of the night and is satisfied.
It listens for footfalls when the dogs bark
in the village in the village in the village.

In the village in the village in the village
life repeats itself, life undoes itself
and then does itself up in the same guise.
We are careful not to fail to repeat
the same salutations, the same farewells
our parents and our parents' parents use.
They are wise, we are small and the day long.
Death comes but once but when it comes to life
no one would be unwilling to repeat
in the village in the village in the village.

THE YAHWEH WORD-WALL

As I galloped through the field I noticed the shadow
of an invisible hand that was painting graffiti
on a great big wall. I was shocked when I sensed the scribble
spelled YAHWEH in every language known to man
so far as I could unscramble the ciphers
that swarmed and danced around across the bricks.
The Rosetta-like screed had the St. Vitus fits.

I approached the barrier with great expectations
but couldn't find a door. A pretty small sign read:
The Great I Am That I Am buckles down on *your* side
of the Great Divide, and the letters kept right on
calling on me in a lot of lingoes all at once.
I sang back as loud as I could. Then they
stopped, so I stopped. The silence grew like a noiseless bomb.

All the sounds had shifted into an idle in neutral
the way all colors puddle together to make white.
It was all so absurd it made total sense, when
the frozen wall boiled away like hot ice, and Zounds!
the smoke drifted off, and behind and before
me was exactly the same green pasture at both
wall-gone ends of the self-justifying horizon
as the Sun went down banging its golden gong.
My horse shook his head, gave a "Well I'll be" kind of a snort,
and since it was impossible to go back to when
we started out, we continued into the future
hoping for good luck, good fortune, and happy times.

THE WITCHDOCTOR'S SHUFFLE

He's a dust devil whirling around in a leopard-skin rag.
He pogos up n down; he blows in the wind like a paper bag.
He pixies in moon dust and the cauldron shoots caps
off like a starting gun as chromosome champs
pass the baton on gen to gen as they run
relays millions of years old and then some to kingdom come.

Shooting through Hubble's barrel of light years,
can we rearrange history if we wormhole nearer
to the start? If plasma hadn't divested,
would we have invested? Hope the decadent past
won't infect the visions of the future still intact
as fast as forefathers faded to fiction from fact.

Out of an anonymous miasmal froth, a child went forth
into a world of graveyards & names. She spoke of a new testament
whose rhymes pop in a nouny air next to verbs giving us the when,
though it's always just now even if we're looking back then.

THE HIPPO'S HEAD

The hippo's head would not fit on a platter.
So Doug and the boys carried it by the ears
to the biology lab where we skinned it.
A mountain of flab and flesh, with a mouth
like a clothes chute, it chased a washer-woman
down the main street; later collapsed like a cliff
to the game warden's bead at the foot of town.

The whole school gathers to watch the scalpel
scrape the plastic mask from skull and jawbone.
The magnitude of tissue shifts the lesson
on life to an engineering feat.
The pupils' eyes dilate, larynxes laugh
as the grotesque labia loosen, the pores
replete with toothbrush bristles, the skin smooth
and rubbery. As we finish, a voice scatters
our hypnotized ring of eyes and hands, calls down
from the house, "Hippo steaks are done!"

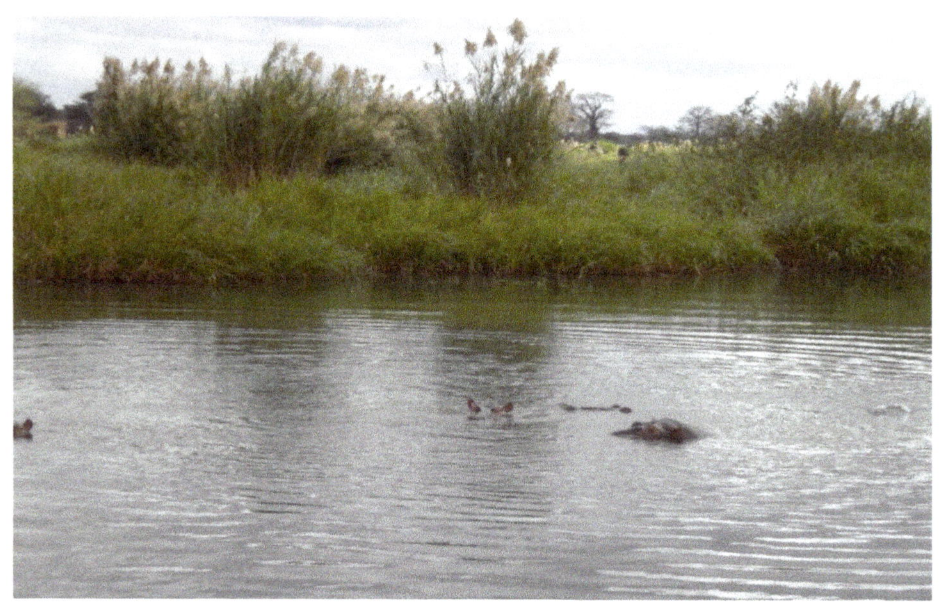

Hippos Swimming Photo by Lance Cole

SECOND NIGHT WITH THE WITCHDOCTOR

Fire & brimstone draped in leopard-skin mantle pinches
in poisonous powders and the cauldron bubbles.
Inside the fumes you see a new kind of baby is born
under the melancholy eye of the lunatic moon.

In Hubble's barrel of light years we shoot through
the bore back to Beginning's expletive-deleted explosion.
Volatile eons later our star is reflexive in our
reflecting on the fact that if the Sun hadn't devolved
we wouldn't have evolved. Let's hope the I-told-you-so Past
won't abandon us to his Digger O'Dell galaxies that're
tombstones by the time they shock our eyesight with insight.

In the witchdoctor's vapors we see the primordial child
is looming, her mutable eyes counting on gamma rays,
her tongue bubbling over with scenarios to scribble down.
The drama she casts is a spell in deed as well as word
since words without deeds do not to heaven go.
Talking, copytalk n soul, the sacred Big Three, began
their trek in Africa, so listen up, get a life,
and dobe dobe do; jazz up like a bird and scat free.
Otherwise, "read *The New Yorker*, trust in God, and take short views."
Worship the stars in Hollywood and believe in the evening news.

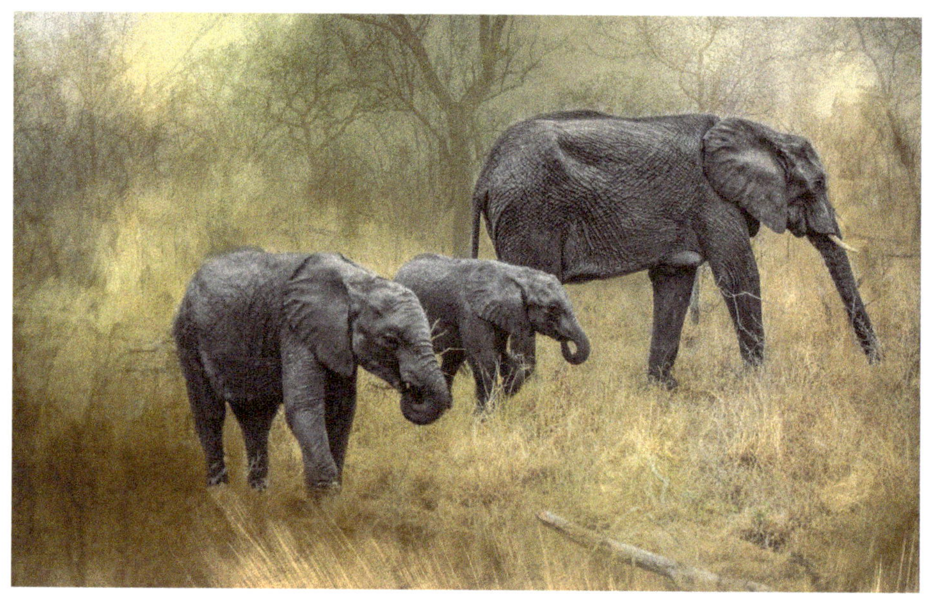

Ellies in grass Photo by Carol Leadbetter

IV

African Haiku

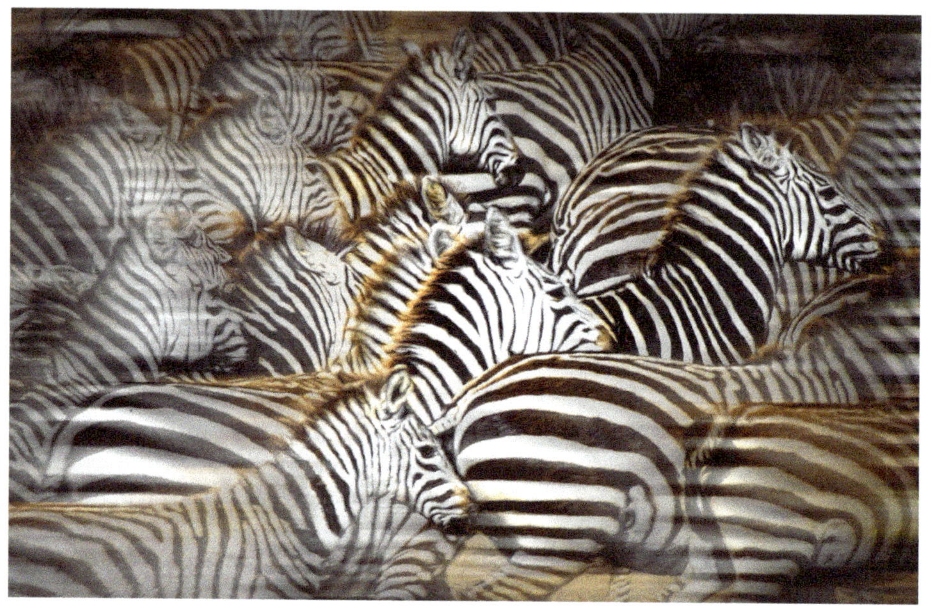

Zebras on plains Photo by Carol Leadbetter

TB Ward

The x-rays resemble Andromeda's
blizzard exploding the chest.

ADDIS AT EASTER

Goats flung over their shoulders
like Italian sweaters,
Ethiopians throng Addis at Easter.

The women wear white cotton dresses
and have gorgeous faces.

In the souk we adjust each other's price.
Walk away, walk back again
until the deal is struck
to start the day
with a stroke of good luck.

MOUNT MALAWI

To a clash of cymbals and roll of drums
the sun comes up like thunder
over Mozambique across the plains.

But tonight we dance to the gossiping drums
of Mbona the rain giver,
who quenches the fiery red thirst of the sun.

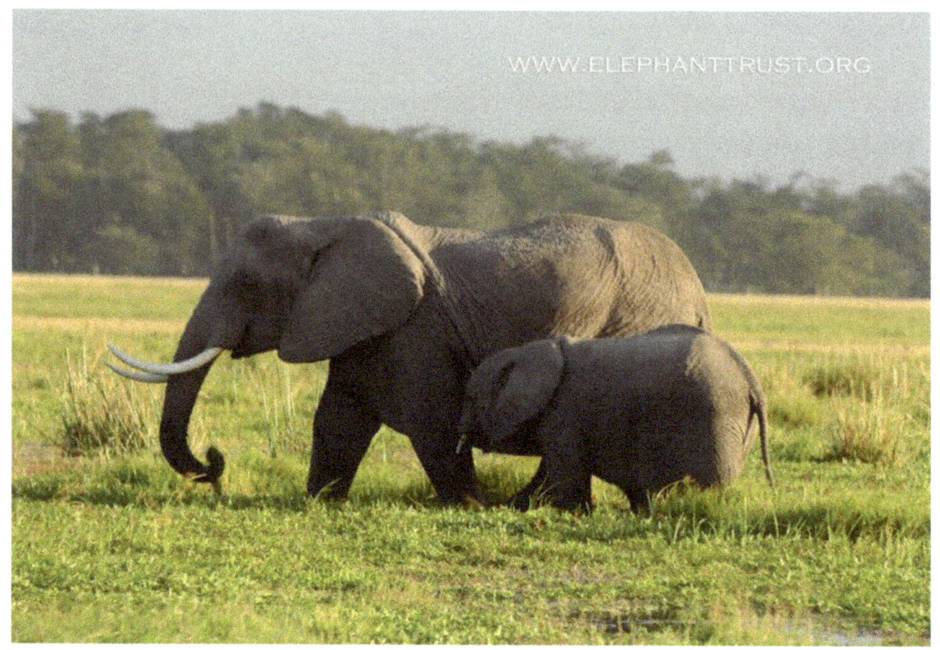

Dawn in the Highlands Photo by Cynthia Moss

DAWN IN THE HIGHLANDS

In the little river
under the melting diamond
of the morning star,
we swim and sway.

Then dawn flings the night
behind its shoulders
and the moon reluctantly gives way.

LEGEND IN A YAHWEH CAVE

These dry bones inhabit the abomination
of the desolation of the abandonment of motion.
Here's a scabrous pouch of weather-parched leather
ponchoing a mangy blotch of skin n bones.
I bend over this unholy collapse of a Romanesque
apse of a skull and ruined choir of ribcage
but I still can't decipher the mortal message
emanating from the cavities that once were eyes.

Turning from the chalky calculus
of this excavation site remorseless as death,
I feel like I'm Balboa's wild surmise
as in my Darien thicket I surprise
a vixen's widowed eyes blazing like rhyme
through the dark apportionments of past time.

NOMADS

Here is wherever sleep unfolds their tent.
Now is forever dragging its steps behind them.
The future's a dust devil whirling them forward.

THE BARRAGE

1. We compare the hole we dug
to the level field that was there before.

2. The excavation exchanges itself
for cloudbursts and a looking glass of water
doubling the view at the end of the wet
season with a cloudless blue sky returning.

3. The rain eliminated the hole that comes back
in proportion to how well the crops do
considering how many melted diamonds we pump out,
and crocodiles won't drink from our bloodstream
since we don't need their river anymore.

V

The Game Park

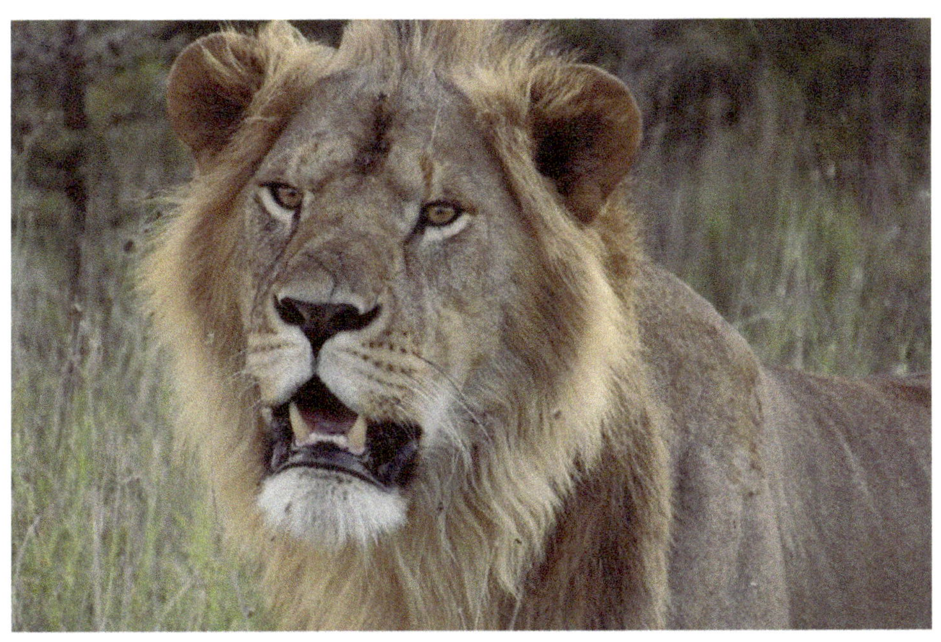

Photo by Cynthia Moss, Amboseli Elephant Trust

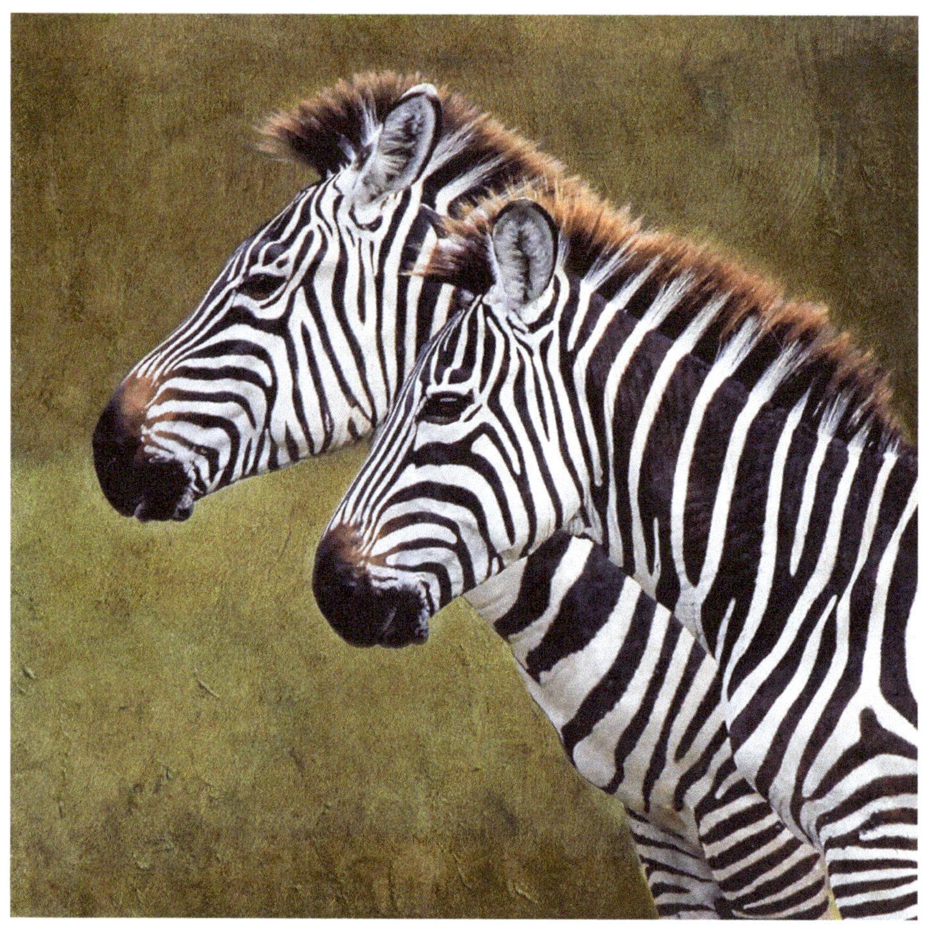

Zebras Photo by Carol Leadbetter

GORILLA IN GLASS

My shaggy heart rages in a big glass box
caught in the web of sidewalks and highways
that lead to the zoo on Sunday afternoons.
The tigers doze in an artificial
habitat complete with a pool and some trees,
in their eyes a hard, indifferent blaze.

Visitors pause to gape, and then drift on
past screaming macaws and rutting baboons,
but always an audience for him,
the bad boy and clown, who never gives up
trying to break loose. His elbow beats
bellicose on the glass before he retreats

to sulk in a corner. There he broods inside
himself, nine hundred pounds of blazing hate
within a little mountain of glossy black.
The children tease him back to the fore,
and for a moment those crew-cut eyes sweep
from face to face, showing the fury they keep

against his invisible cage. The hairy
elbow bangs the bulletproof glass again:
A loud stillness surrounds us, then shatters
into peals of laughter as he turns to shuffle
back n forth in his cube, in which is crammed
all that anyone could know of the damned.

LOVE IN A TENT IN AFRICA

Skin the color of sun, and the sun
the color of skin collecting the golden
vitamin of D in a human bottle
of harvested sunlight warming the skin
of love: Love, love me in the sun skin to skin.
Be the fruit of the vine condensed in a bottle
and I will drink until thoroughly golden
inside and out, I mistake us for the sun.

Under wraps the body frets to be free,
to be a me that is you, so be thou me.
Clothing deceives, distorts the meaning
of the skin. Against such corruption, your kindness
is as radical as our nakedness.
My longing for you is the only meaning
in the world. I cannot contain it in me.
Breathing outward into you I am free.

Your breathing quiets me in the quiet
breathtaking night, night striped as always
with Venetian slats of sight across your
eyes blinking to the nearby blinking neon gas.
Our bodies laugh they are so glad. The grass
of our grave will grow over us in waves but your
touch is my shore of resurrection. Always
our hands are so intrigued the world lies quiet.
You're a golden girl genie in a bottle
of skin and your naked kindness always frees
a grass-like quietness in me as the sun
blows its golden gases across our eyes.

LIONESS DINING

Her beard bristly as tufts in a dry field,
Blondie sips from deep vermilion wells
that life in melt keeps brimming with blood.
Her barbeque grill of fangs lights its grid.
She shakes her muzzle and the sparks fly.
Her hot-wired eyes short out when the tines
of her teeth rake the rawhide n crush
a now-rusty rack of bones in her jowls.
Sneaky hyena backs off n growls.
Interrupt this banquet and lightning attacks.
Corrupt this action and those flaring jets
will zap you with a Buck Rogers death ray.
Now she's on her claws and tearing this way.
Ey! better get back to the Land Rover fast.

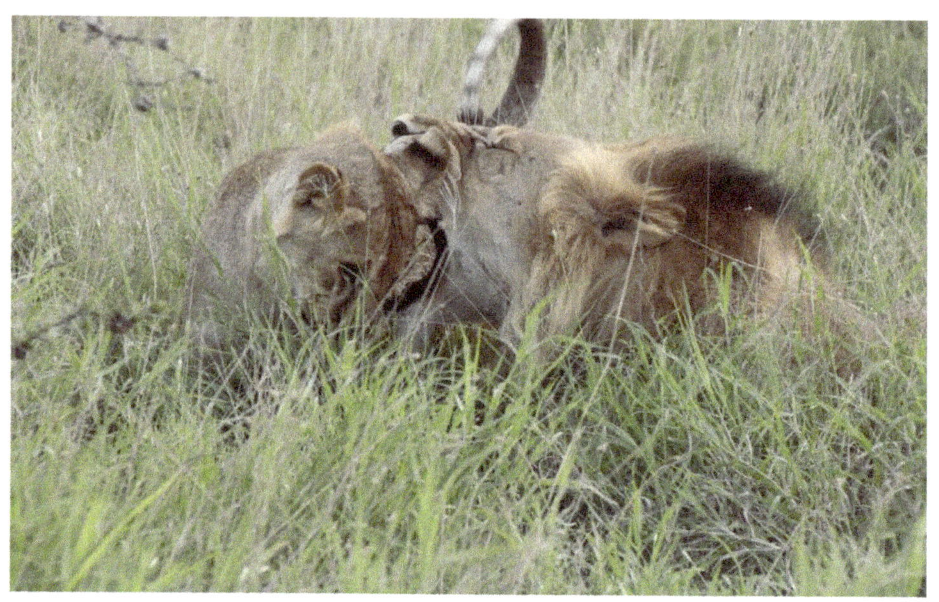

Lioness Dining Photo by Cynthia Moss

NILE CROCODILE

Its tongue slumbers in a cave between stalagmite
and stalactite sabers. Its yawn of fixed bayonets
is a temp control swapping hot for cold,
the beast being poikilothermic rather
than homoeothermic, meaning this lizard
that looks a lot like a giant suitcase, is not
on thermostat control. Its world spindles
round a hungry heart that lurks to snap up
a footstep or for a fin whose Nile perch
will give itself to god. Submarining
more stealthy than U-boats for an hour
at a time, it sneak-attacks anything
that moves, even hulls during the mating season.

Plover and sandpiper peck at the tsetse
flies and leeches on the grizzled leatherbacks,
who were lined up long before we got here,
flossing their teeth on Nile cotton sunbeams.

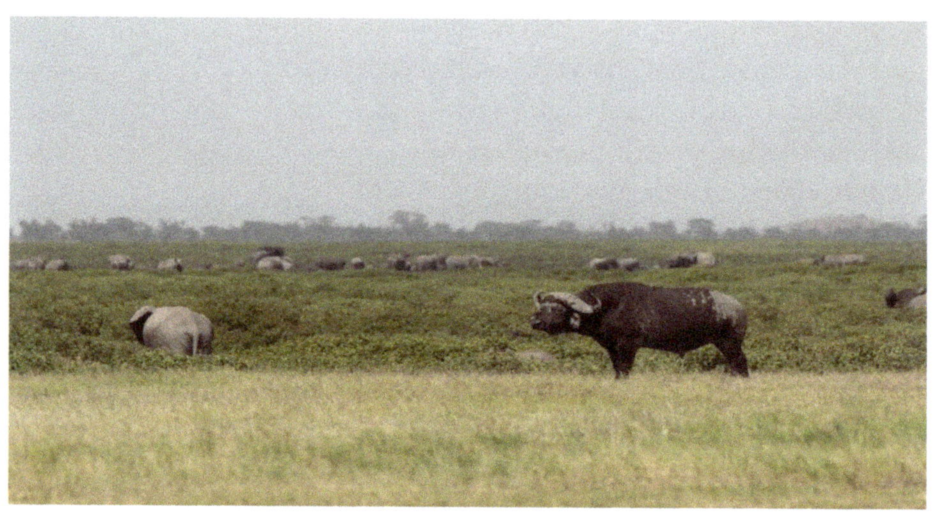

Amboseli Game Park Photo by Cynthia Moss

AMBOSELI GAME PARK

The heat presses everything down in place
except for the trembling herringbone heat waves.
The only rupture in the shimmy-n-shake stillness
is from the slow-motion rollercoastering
giraffes loafing through acacia leaves,
and a lounging lioness's flyswatter tail.
Along the horizon in the fragile distance
mobs of zebra and wildebeest are shaving
their own herd's five-o'clock shadow as they nibble
their way across the plain's be-stubbled face.

Here the colors are like weathered thatch,
dishwater-blond, buckwheat honey, and urine,
as if the sun had gilded all things great n small
and then tarnished them with time. Rolling over,
the lioness lifts a hungry eye and swipes
at bugs with her paw, and grunting dives again
into her tawny field of dreams. Land Rovers
infested with tourists track along the slim
trajectory of laterite trails. We dine
on life to live, and every bone's a wish
absorbed in the universe from which it came.
First comes the dish and then comes the wish,
according to Bertie, who lent me this line.

MY ARMS IN OUR AFRICAN TENT

I bend my arms and elbows in a hoop
and your flashback jumps insomniac sheep
through my slightly left-handed lopsided loop
as I float on my back in a half-empty bed.
Your absence is the doughnut's essential hole
that gives it its identity-making soul.

The fork of the new moon hooks like a bull,
gores the matador's black velvet cape of night
vast for being more lonely than the day.
My body gropes till I'm down to appendages
and shoulders as if my brain had gone missing
and I'm a headless horseman groping for his mind,
or a bowlegged cowboy's arms-raised figure eight,
also without sombrero or cabeza.

My arms have nothing to hold but nothing's
intense vacuum. I thought I was in levitation
when I held you. My arms rose of themselves
straight up like the perpetually groping flares
of candles teaching my pupils to see
but all they glimpse is that my memories
people the peepholes of my eyes with you.

At last, the sunshine melts the night's dark wax.
Dawn announces your on-time arrival
and you roll down the runway of the sun
so we can plug the doughnut and make one bun.

PHEROMONE HIGH ON THE HIGH PLAINS

As is the habit of certain mating birds,
we spit-shoot more pebbles on top of the rest
for the perfect pyramid of times gone by,
whose apex rises to every occasion
by building the basis for the next one
and so on, so every Now's capstone gets buried
beneath a mound of petrified moments
that keep on piling on top of each other.

After the pheromone stage, he argues it
didn't matter and won't swab the latrine.
His irritations won't induce a pearl.
The gleam now is just a soap bubble popping.
What could have happened thins to a shadow
following him like a dog in daylight.
He goes to the darkness to get rid of it.
For some weeks he wears the mask of sorrow
and reads sad stories about the death of kings.

THE NIGHTFISHERS OF DAKAR

The nightfishers are stealthy like
shadows. They flutter like black ribbons
through the lamplight's reflections.
Picasso gave them daytime colors at Antibes.
What a draftsman he was! He could make
squiggles come alive. The light smears itself
Monet-like across the fishermen's faces,
that are innocent of such art. They fish
for fish in the darkness with a knowledge
they have acquired in the day, or do they have
a feeling for the velvety blindness
that the rest of us lack? In their veto
of dazzle and spangle, they glide
gondola-like past glittering
lamps shaking an electrical confetti
on fathoms of not fur or feathers
but of coruscating scales, adagios
of scales that balance the centuries
of domination by the land
as they take in the life-giving oxygen
through the grinning pump of their gills.
The nightfishers are friends with your shadows
since they themselves have learned to be shadows.
They respect the ancient give n take
between dark n light, sea n sky
so they can dart in between and make a living.

VI

Subsaharan Adventures

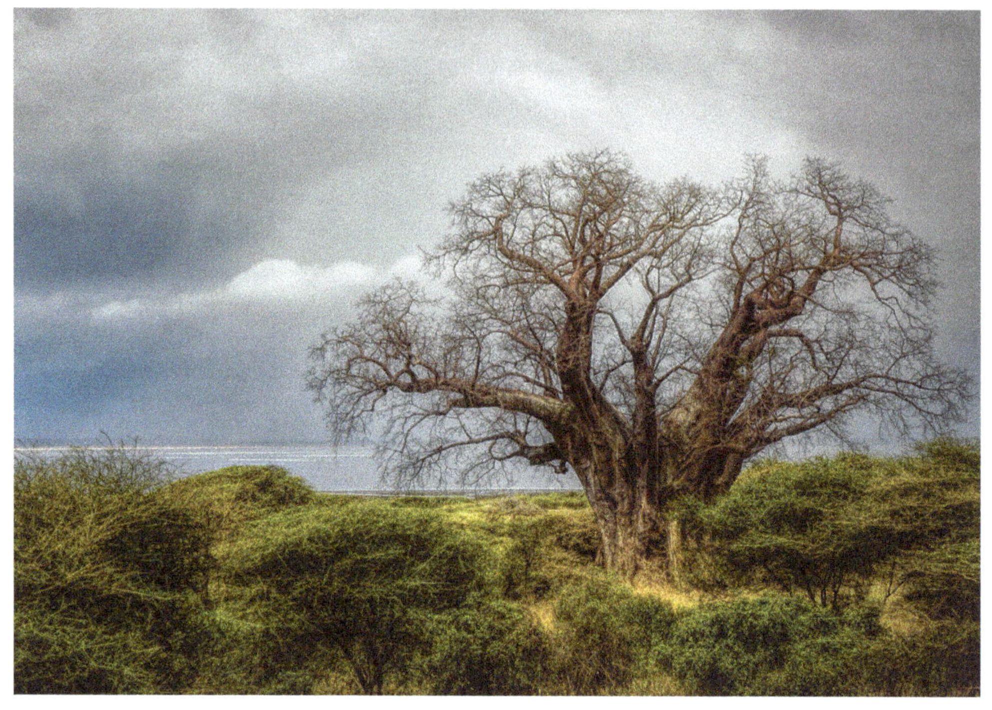

Baobab tree 2 Photo by Carol Leadbetter

"UPSIDE-DOWN TREE," THE BAOBAB #1

It can suck in its bark to hollow a cave,
and sunshine smears butter for fifty feet
on its big fat baked-potato skin.
When leaves peel in the dry season, its legs
and arms would look the same if x-ray eyes
could see the bottom as well as the top.
With branches swirling like the limbs of figure
skaters, maybe its roots are radial also.

Here's a combination water tank
and fruit tree in arid regions of Africa
when you are in need of moisture and food.
Its hippo-thick hide founds a neighborhood
physical and spiritual savings bank
where moisture hides its treasure from the sun,
where bodies deposit their shadows at noon,
withdrawing them with interest before dusk,
and where the Rain God Mbona brews the storm.

Dawn beams its lantern across the baobab's
upside-down wisdom-tooth watchtower, against which
the locomotive past, and the future in form
of the always tardy Ilala Steamer,
are both measured and found equally wanting.
This tree was born in the same year as Christ,
here where the Sapient Blues Band did its first gig.

UPSIDE-DOWN TREE #2

Between similar-looking roots n branches
stands the thickest, most gnarled elephant's foot
with melted cheese on it, the stalk imploding
into concavities, though sometimes the bark bulges
in a burl that curls upward n sags lower. Dry season,
its arms look the same as its roots' feet whirling
around in the soil like the radial
finale of an Olympic skater. And,
the tree may be more antique than Methuselah,
or Ulfilas' Gothic text in Uppsala.

The trunk is a combination water tank
and fruit tree in arid zones in Africa.
Its gourd-like fruit tastes fair to okay
when you're tired n hungry. Its warty, scarred but
elegant beige hide, hides the comfortable spirit
of hearth, home, and neighborhood.
So here's a kind of physical/spiritual bank
wayfarers rely on as they eclipse like shadows
at high noon when there are no shadows, or glide
by in cloaks of starlight when fires are burning
in n out of the eyes of medicine men,
casting shadows through the moody depths of night.
The shadows flicker on hut-walls, n tree trunks
that're high, wide, n handsome as a watchtower.
Their cross-sections rise pillar-like
loaded with inscrutable endorsements
from the spirits who reside inside of
these columns only a Dali could imagine,
proving once again that fact is stranger than fiction.

NIGHT TRAIN TO KISUMU

The Moon inhales its own dope,
exhales chimney soot and Ivory soap.
The dining car enlivens its mirrors
with white linen napkins and a silver service.
Jolly good food and fine French wine
extend the evening past bedtime
and history's untold mysteries.

Swimming the train's electrical eel
through the molasses of night,
its male intention, which is Time,
passes through fallopian resistance,
which is Space, to reach its destination,
the future our home, or is it?
Home is where things come to visit
till you fail to resist the urge to move on.

The train says: "Might as well accept it;
there are boats, there are cars
but they're merely the means to an end,
an excursion without a style.
The best fix is my stable axle
round which the crankshaft never fails
and my wheels always follow the rails.
Besides, Kisumu does not exist,
does not even want to exist
until you arrive there,
though by land you cannot pass it.
Stretch it out as long as you can."

Then the conductor gives us the real time:
That's all, folks, end of the line.

MONROVIA

Rusty tin roofs propped up by skinny black elbows as if on the sticks
of dotty pier stakes, twiggy arms stretched high above twisty-
tight scalps as if pressing barbells to new heights
and clutching the rafters to keep them from flapping away in windshear
and that's Monrovia's shantytown as I remember it
and loved it for better or worse in good times and in bad.

Muddy, my spirits dark n dreary in the *dreckische*
fuss of the rainy season, I waded around floating on
the murmuring waves of our walky-talky breath as
authentic as the salty-dog diction of the pounding surf.

I was a beggar at the gate of your stick-in-the-mud haven,
imploring you to save me from my CPA* over-computerized self.
Let the world come here to learn how simple it is to live.
I snuck through your gate to share your tough times
since suffering is the second-most real thing in the world.
Though the rain brings rust, it's the elixir of life
so let it all come down; let the dirt mix n make mud.
I love you, Monrovia; live and all manner of things may be well.

*Continuous Partial Attention, a re-wiring of the brain due to
extended exposure to video games, computers, and IT devices.

THE TOTEMS OF THE HOTEL IVOIRE

The shadows of these tall up-and-down statues climb
the infinitely expanding dimensions of night.
They preside over the transience of the flesh.
They guard the majesty of the air.
They are the aristocracy of the dust.
Meanwhile, the horizontal swimming pool
is a necessary tool for attracting tourists
whose hearts click to the roll of roulette, whose hands
cut the deck for luck, and whose palms are frangipanis'
fragile petals, shallow, scented, and white,
but the statues are deep and dark like the night.
They have come here to tell us something about
the tall peaks of darkness and their jungle-bird stars.
Look in their eyes; they have strange things to tell you.

LAMU

Sinbad sailed past sea serpents to Africa
and back on trade winds to palaces.
He loaded ivory that clattered in the hold.
Also gold and leather. Maybe he found Lamu.
The only way still to get there is by dhow.
Then the traveler forgets to go back
for so long he exiles the rest of the world.

Gradually Lamu was abandoned
in the waters of an eternal past.
Its ruins became ruins that had
always been ruins, ruins protected
by the curious skin of time gone by,
which holds our sense of ourselves together.
Sometimes the skin hardens into the shells
of unageing places: Lamu, Lhasa, Katmandu.

It's too much trouble to go to Lamu
unless you're in love with the past that made you
into something that has to go beyond it
unless you dig the ruins so completely
you burrow through them to another time
when cities aged in character like the sun,
avoiding the death of everything new.

BUG OFF! Lake Malawi

When flies get stuck
in the goo of their gossip,
flypaper twisting in the wind,
their buzz goes bananas.

In the deep freeze of Time
their bother is fossilized
when their bodies are magnified
in the glue of the resin
stiffening to forever amber.

Webster's defines "life" as "not dead."
That's brilliant. I'd say life is light's
parasite similar to what bugs are to us,
though we can turn that around when
we feed protein-rich lake flies
with fifty percent protein
to babies dying from kwashiorkor
on the shores of Lake Malawi.

In the battle between bugs n people
Mamas would harvest the insects,
waving their baskets around
in figure-eight, butterfly motions,
then squashing the bugs into crunchy wads
for the protein-deficient babies.
So who's eating who now, old sock?
Whatever. The nature of creeps
is they bug you:
Buzz off! Shoo, fly, shoo.
Spring is sprung, the grass is riz,
I wonder where my flyswatter is.
Smack! Got 'em.

NORFOLK HOTEL, Nairobi

When Teddy and Ernie sat here gut-sucking up the gin
& tonics, they tickled the air's ears with burly tall tales
for the most part true. Mustachioed mouthpieces they were,
though it no longer matters that much since they're dead now.

So now we sit here soaking up the gin & tonics, too, but
that won't qualify us for the same big-stick adventures
so we'll make things up as we go along while sitting here.
If you go out and try it for yourself, you may step on a cobra
and a leopard ate a waiter the other day as simple as that.
So you sit here on the woody wouldabeen verandah dreaming of
the olden days when men were bold and excuses weren't
invented and there was real jeopardy and you made
a difference in the lives of those who survived
their adventures in those life-or-death encounters
when you grow or die without expectations and make
yourself more buzzed than survival itself and that's
the way it was for Buffalo Bill now defunct, for Ernest
Hemingway, F. Scott Fitzgerald, Teddy R. the President,
and others who still live in Africa right now where you
feel more alive than you do in the rest of the world at large.
And yes I was here in Nairobi during the coup attempt.
The Norfolk manager gave us room & board for free so we
quipped: There's a lot of cooing but no billing going on
around here, ha ha ha. That story's true; some others not.
C'est moi, not Moi.

REFUGEES

She wears oily rags and her birthmark face
is pummeled flat as a stomped-on squashed beer can.
Home is heel to sole, heel to sole,
the rain her wrap, the sun her stole,
I mean her shawl, that's all.

In Africa, monsoons rain down whole hogs
instead of cats and dogs.
The house of mud holds on
to its tin-roof hat,
for floods could beat him flat
and sweep him miles away.

The heat's so thick it becomes a screen.
Motion slows to a few frames per scream,
between each step, the fraction of a flash,
as a lost traveler signals
with a mirror through a magnifying glass.

They march through yesterday.
Weather erodes their backs
and mind gives no reflection
as they vanish in their tracks.
Refugees just fade away.

Need thickens their skin
whose birth certificates have never been.
Whited out, pressed too thin,
their number's unsensed by the census.
Their time has no more tenses.

Whatever you are has come as far
as the convergence of our star
and the DNA's narrowing
down-to-you-only arrow in a bulls eye.
But refugees come from nowhere
and they just fade away.

Alas, the losses before we arrive
at a place where we can live,
though Lazarus says,
just being alive is being home,
but not without a roof and wall
and only skin and bone.

Heat waves are a memory bank
recording the same thing as before.
Walking forward is walking backward
like Marcel Marceau, Marcel Marceau
going nowhere with nowhere to go.

You will never see them again.
Refugees just fade away.

OLD FEZ

Go down to this den of antiquity
and you'll see vegetable dyes in vats
for staining hides, and tap-tapping tools
workers tinkered with in the tenth century.
Nearby, the first university ever
was founded by a woman. Now it's a mosque
whose filigree is holy calligraphy.
Down the alley there's the oldest library
with parchments rescued from Alexandria
where fires took a big bite out of history.

To spy on these streets abandoned by Time
is discovering a past that was a
thousand years napping. Do these mind-molds
that shaped our psyche hold residual value
in a cultural subconscious? Or are they
broken up and completely abandoned
whenever a new culture is formed?
If no more cultures can be invented
because there are no more alternative sources,
and all cultures have to die as they lived,
museum cultures will have to survive us.

Ancient places are to be visited,
though we would never want to live on streets
you can't drive a medium-sized car through even.
But maybe we've neglected the victory
only possible when we run a reverse,
and back-pedaling, fading back, and waiting
for the present to spread the future's defenses,
we uncork an everlasting Hail Mary pass.
It floats in the air, and falls in good hands.

SONG OF THE UNENDING SILENCE, Liberian Rainforest

Rainforests shingle their roofs with leaves that leave us
speechless on the grounds we've deepened the silence's
ban on clamor till it's still as the hum of telephone wires
though in this case no telephone wires are present
so the stillness is even more outspoken.

We glide through the cloud-prone columns that groove on
their own bark, and we're guided by a hush that
surrounds us with its canopy umbrella. The stillness
is a huge sound-sock tugged inside-out into no-noise
the way white is all shades toppled outside-in.
So stillness is all sounds cancelling each other out
as it recapitulates the phylogeny of the late great
Mute Button State when Antimatter's amphitheater of
a silence of less than nothing bombed into everything.

Here, Time-past brakes at the black hole of NOW, that
is the only time-zone that stays the course. In the dim,
dispersed light, wave after wave of photons blink
through the blade-nets. Their flash is too fast to be seen.
It shorts out in the air's eyes, yet it makes
the visible possible, and the whole scene's a "WOW,"
like a lot of palindromes in that it has a midpoint
whose forward and backward cast the same spell as
if Life's motion picture progress towards death reached
a balance point here, where, though the reel rolls on,
at the same time it seems to spin backwards through memory
towards birth. So this may be the moment when birth and death
are balanced, and this great hush is the level bubble
shaped like an O, and it whispers, "O, you should understand
you stand in the first & last cathedral in the world
where a woodwind quartet plays the Song of the Unending Silence
from before and after there was anything else at all.
Everything that ever was & is to be, is here now.

MERMAID IN ZANZIBAR

On a salty shore on the isle
slumps the stranded dugong.
The sun strops its blue blade
on her flank, but still
the sack of her rubbery skin
contrives to hold the raw flesh in,
though meat leaks through lips
where ever-rude propellers
poached her length and strength.

The shore sickles its waves
continually: Its harvest
keeps threshing her tail
along a windrow of spine.
Pectoral flippers hang down
limp as paws, and her snout,
blunt and blind as a mole's,
nudges its shadow on the sand.

The ocean rejected her
and she will never return
to barge through stained glass windows
in the liquid cathedral
of the brine's crepuscular vaults.
Death will keep her heretic and here,
rocked on this beach
till her shipwrecked ribs
buttress the low-flying air,
snagging a flag of seaweed
that used to be her flowing hair.

THE BLOWFISH

It was on a beach near Beira
where we first saw him being brought
in on a spear by a skin diver.
He was a useless catch, not good
for eating, so was abandoned
on the beach with his bloated lips
open; still alive. He had blown
his spiked skin up like a balloon,
and his Charles Laughton face told nothing.

That was months ago, but we can
yet visualize him, who by now
is only a stiff pouch on the
bleached salt wash, but has become
a symbol to us of all pointless
suffering; though perhaps he did
not suffer much; perhaps merely
a faint feeling of suffocating
in dead air, with nothing to do

but puff out his sides to look somewhat
larger than he really was.
Also at the same shore were a man
who sat sucking a pipe in his yawl,
and a woman searching for lobster.
But all that we can remember
distinctly is the blowfish swelling
beneath a palm, and how ugly
he was, which made the difference.

VII

Nilotic Dreams

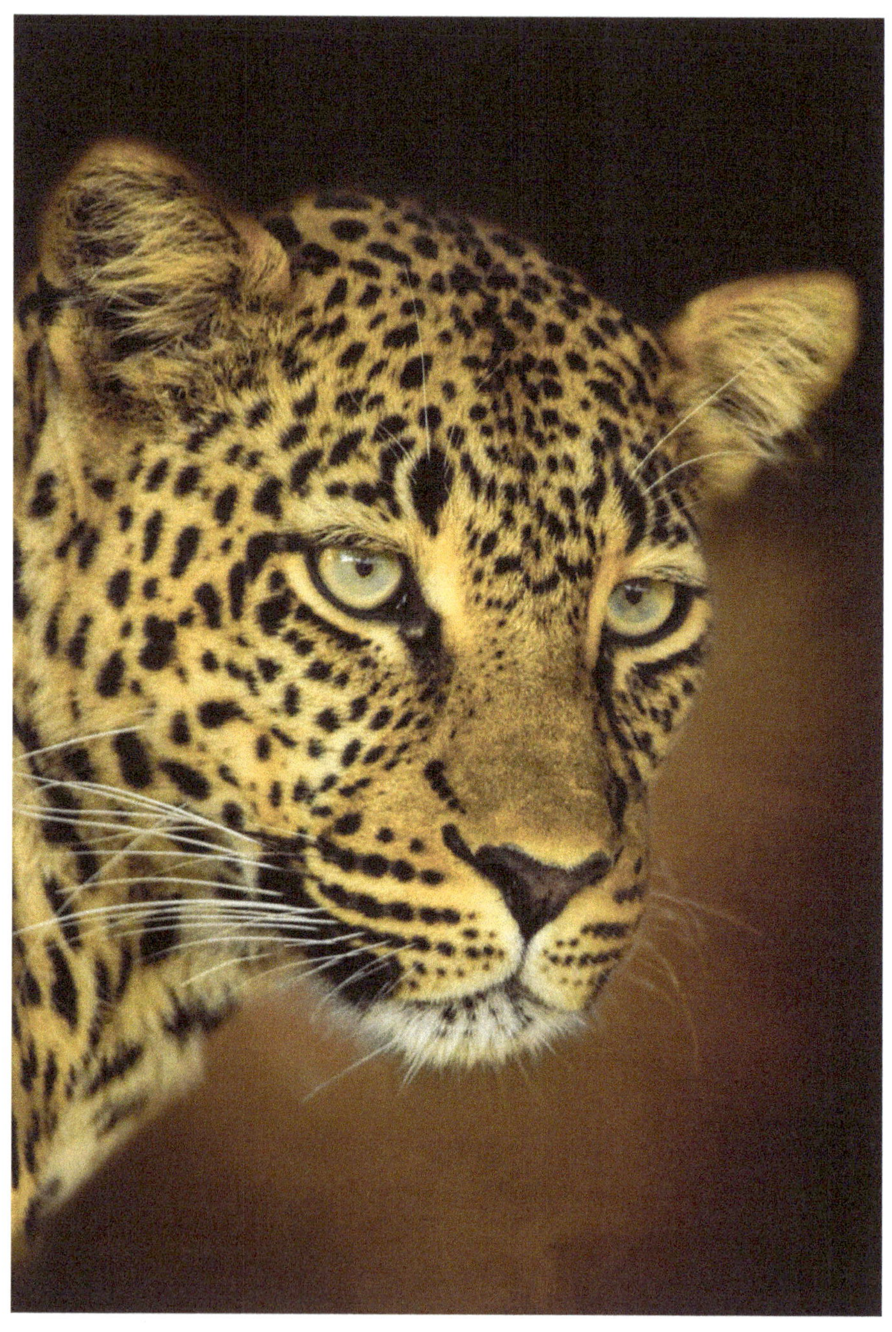

Leopard portrait Photo by Carol Leadbetter

GIZA AT THE MINT

On top of Old Giza all covered with dust
the capstone was stolen and smuggled out west
onto the backside of U.S. dollar bills where the crest
is now a never-sleeping, all-seeing iris-burst.

From this AWOL cap, if you climb to the dizziest rock
you see the desert elastic as eternity here
represented by the buzzard's widespread finger-like wingtips.

And here one can peep through History's backward-looking retro-
spective telescope at the nubile dancers of the harem's
hootchie-kootchie of bubbles & foam. One sees dust devils rising
from the sand and collapsing into time-baking mummy-crumbs.

Giza is so voluminous I used to climb to the lopped-off tip
of the stoned paradigm to peek over its decapitation to where
heat waves dance the dune-wave in all directions, wow! Now it's
an abandoned desert that was once an abundant garden.

Cosmonauts can see these three titanic tetras
from outer space: Here I am guys; I'm waving
my red white & blue T-shirt at your space capsule.
Can't you see it? I'm perched on the platform of the missing big top

that got mass-produced on the backs of greenbacks for Uncle
Sam via a graven image and a Gringo-green dye,
and that's the way it is here at the Fed
minting like made for u & for me—reflections on a glowing eye.

THE SUN KINGDOM, Abu Simbel

Rising and setting sun look like a candled egg yolk
at the juncture when they choose sides on the skyline
to hatch an albumin-like cloud or sink to a dark time.
Based on elemental, sub-atomic evidence us chickens
are the brood of flame-feathered Buff Orpington hens.
Amazing, that sunshine can masquerade as bowers bee
lined with flowers.

Do finicky sounds between larynx and tympanum repeating
the syllable "sun" persuade the seminal source
to be more real than he actually is, magnified, of course
as many times as we burble another "sun" sound out
now we know light is basically what life is all about?

Was African dusk the photo filter photosynthesizing
the meta-bionic, distributive fuel cell we call "soul"?
At dawn and dusk, between question and answer, half n whole,
enter the twilight zone when peripheral vision sees best
that ends are cliffs where fledglings hollow the nest.
So be thou bi-modal as twilight, the instant your shadow blends
into, or back from, darkness like the Magnificent Whirling Ampersand
who links us to strangers who think with us hand in hand.

KARNAK

The heat waves look like a Jean Harlow blondie-wig on the run,
scuttling along similarly-scalloped smoky dunes
of which there's a surplus in these particular time zones.

At Karnak the incense would cobra up from a smoke pot and
then the vernal equinox would tell peasants when to plant
peanuts
for goober-good crops for to renew the empire at large and export
too.

The priests' cotton gowns were lunar moths in love with sunshine
and the clerical chorus lobbied for more glamorous days.
What if twilight condemned the day to darkness forever? So
they chanted with might & main their songs of exhortation.
They'd already singed their eyelashes on sunrays but their eye-
brows
were capable of predicting optimal times to plant n harvest
and read special spatial arrangements in the sky. They saw
measurement & proportion would be of Pythagorean significance.

I feel humbly at home among these vertiginous erections.
I Sméagol to the altar where X marked the hot spot for
the vernal equinox, and the resurrected Osiris would
shoot a skinny laser of light onto the bulls eye's cross-
hairs and this would throw out the lifeline of hope.
All this makes my promiscuous ignorance more acceptable
as I stand awe-fully under these pillars propping up the sky.

THE KING AND QUEEN OF CIVIL SOCIETY, Karnak

The Nile Delta spidered the wettest web
but left behind the Sahara's silent dead.
It took a listening silence to learn how to talk.
This Queen of the Night, wound in mummy cloth,
stares through her mask like a death's-head moth.

Dipping quills in Night's genius ink well,
star-struck poets pushed conscience over the ledge
to where its bets could no longer be hedged.
Honest Abe split rails right from wrong long after
ten commandments ditched the Red Sea's gathering storm.

The Devil shivered at the Blind Lady's laws
she juggled in hands that once were claws in paws.
Blindfold off, she was fair as love at first dawn.

The Sun King swore an oath: I *never* harmed anyone
nor told a lie; *nor* polluted the waters of the Nile.
He said, "Civilization rests on 'Thou shalt not,'
though my Queen would rather say Yes.
Reality acknowledges zero excuses though human
capacity for rationalization is infinite.
Still, my Queen tips the pan up in favor of Yes
while I bring it down with the judgment of No
for some are 'weighed in the balance and found wanting.'"

Also sprach the Sun King in flaring crown to
his Queen in her blindfold's lightning-white gown.

THE GREAT WING OF NIGHT SOARING ACROSS AFRICA

"Darkness" could be a sneaky, opposite-meaning code word
for an interior species of invisible gloss
in the mutant-friendly fashion of St. John de Cross
in which the deeper he dug in the oscuro,
the lighter grew the burden of the everyday horror.
In darkest Africa we saw the light of words.
They burst our brains and flew from our mouths like birds.

Later, in furrows of paper-white earth,
letters sowed black seeds that bloomed into a birth
of mythical monsters in a virtual froth.
Myrmidon warriors are barracked in dictionaries.
Armies will have to besiege our academies
to uproot these sandbagging mercenaries.

Africa's a night in which you're as good as blind,
your words as real as you know them to be.
Even deities in a phosphorous heaven
shine too dimly to make for blasphemous mind.
You grope towards the rest house by emotional Zen
as Night's calamitous creatures ride tooth n fang on in.
In the night sky of Africa, the comet
of words lit our minds bright as day at night.

MORE AFRICAN NIGHTS

If African nights could be read, it'd be by Braille.
Even suns in the planetarium's plasma-punctured visual
are so remote we can't blaspheme against installations
in the cosmos called the godly constellations.

You grope your way towards the where-can-it-be rest house whose
kerosene lantern has lost its fiery fuse.
Night's calamitous creatures love most the weakest ruse;
like the Zen Master called Life, they brook no excuse,

Hyenas and a cobra's 40-foot hiss
will kill Bill kindly with fang, not slowly with a kiss.
And so our hands taught our minds to think sharp,
to whittle things down to build them back up with honed edges;
and that's how the tool age took shape & staked out its footage.

AMENHOTEP III AND QUEEN TIYE, Cairo Museum

They're both topped off with a smile so serene
it says more than the Cheshire Cat of History,
who wants us to think he knows more than he does.
History's secret is our minds are too small
and aren't helped a lot by barely-evolved languages
only some tens-of-thousands-of-years old.
That's one small tick in the arithmetic of Time
whereas faces have talked face-talk for ages.

Face-talk is a universal language
and these two found a sculptor who was
able to tell their story in lasting stone.
There are not many expressions whose
messages resist erosion for centuries.

Queen Tiye's grin is so contagious
its crease is an <u>in</u>crease that feigns to look
like the new moon with the old one in its arms.
It's as if she could leak the sun's secrets
with a kind of lunar insouciance
that allows her to get away with it
because of the star that shows in her eyes
when the rest of us only see stars in the dark.

NEFERTITI, Berlin-Dahlem

Your profile makes everything screech to a halt.
You could teach the twilight to linger.
You're as cool as Tiffany-colored glass
knocking the daylights out of natural-born sunsets
and glowing for as long as memory
shines its light on your unforgettable face.

Because it's clear you always get it right,
you have the world's most credible face.
We'd never know it by the copies that clog the shops.
Some things can't be replicated.
There are subjects never become objects.
Grammar declines them to objects, yet they are not
and so prove language to be deceitful,
except for Poetry, that Houdinis out of
the cage of syntax and its chain-link phrases.
Rhythm, image, and sound are harp-like bridges
connecting the word-world to the one of being.
Think of Nefertiti's smile also as a time-
binding magic suspension bridge. It spans thousands
of years from her left cheek to your right one right now.

VOYAGE TO THE SUN AND BACK

1.THE GREAT PYRAMID AND THE SUNBOAT, for the Sun King

Giza, Night

While no one's watching, Darkness tip-toes over the top
of Horizon's treadmill and spins us downside-up
into nightshade. The *hoi polloi* picnic here
in a worship mindless therefore probably true.
They are the slaves who scaled these heights and
still support the brunt of potentates and kings.

Next Morning

Dawn's fog pads away on pussy-cat feet.
I perch in an elbow of the big rock magic mountain
and survey the seismic wreckage of yesterday
and the persistence of tomorrow morning.
Seconds drip sandily down the escarpment,
a secret, slow-motion waterfall visible
to those who concentrate on time gone by,
such as these poor pilgrims counting on the first rays.
They are brain cells of the Sun becoming aware of itself.

The Giza-Geezer Speaks

The rugged old geezer strides to light majestically.
Perched on the brink of the present he proclaims,
"These rocks are fireworks now frozen in stone but
aimed like a rocket right back at their shooter the Sun.
Reciprocity's rigged to cheer for its own source
and reflection's one way of telling it like it is,
so though I'm no longer polished, I mirror the sun."
Then the Sun King bellows, "All aboard, we're sailing solar winds!"
And how could he know ankhs should be called photons or
light waves?
And maybe we're just sunflowers on two legs trying
to shinny back up to the radiance we stem from.

2. THE SUN

The sun is the blind eyes of statues gilded
with lilies and fig leaves, the statues cast
of 20-karat gold, and the side frames
and pillars of gold; and the walls mirrors
recollecting gold, and the flashbulbs flashing
to record the slaughter of the camera.

The Aurora Borealis Chimera
whirls into the furnace of its passion,
the twirling red disk of dawn whose semaphore
dots lavender pink and dashes the lame
animal to violet ashes flaking past
the sky-limbs' fried foliage and gutted

scrapers. But it is merely the guided
sediment of reflections in the mirror
at Mt. Palomar. Palomino portions
of the early light crinkle across the lime-
stone tinfoil landscape of the pieced-
together jigsaw puzzle of the past;

and the sky clicks like an ancient camera,
crackles like celluloid, and flames as fast.
A singed circle is left ringing the gilded
eye of the golden body melting the mirror.
It is the sun dissolving everything: Time,
Space, and Fortune in its ferocious fashion.

3. RETURN FROM THE SUN

In the hexahedron of the sun's eye,
the golden honeycomb gilded with mirrors,
my silhouette stalagmite of a cat's eye,
the honey a distillate of the air
scented with buckwheat, the amnesiac
self wakes after a long, indulgent sleep.

Sunlight is so fantastic that who
I am is what I see and what I see
is what I am: glittering interstices
of light glinting through lattice work of gold,
the gold dissolving in anxiety
lest I cannot remember who I was.

Then, am filtered back unto myself
through a widening sieve through which
the world takes on familiarity
again. Am I the world I recognize?
I leave the splendid spider web I failed
to identify as the me I did not know.

LIST OF PHOTOS

All photos by Cynthia Moss, Founding Director, Amboseli Elephant Trust, unless otherwise noted

CONTRIBUTOR NOTES

by Anitra Thorhaug

Andrew Oerke (1932–2013), poet

Andrew grew up in rural parts of the northern central Midwest between the very ancient rolling hills western Wisconsin, with its myriad Lakes, and the flat plains of a drowned ocean in South Dakota and far southern Minnesota. His childhood was full of wilderness adventures of a land recently populated. The pleasures of his boyhood were the birds, the animals and the land itself. His family spent their vacations at the edge of the wilderness beyond Bayfield, Wisconsin on the Chaquamegon Forest and Apostle Islands of Lake Superior. Andrews' happiest memories of his boyhood were in this wilderness. Here he was learned of the bear, wolves, foxes and a variety of animals and plants which easily migrated into northern Wisconsin's dairy land across the frozen winter ice of Lake Superior from the northwestern Ontario's massive primordial forests.

Andrew moved to Texas the second year of college, transferring from St. Olaf's College in Minnesota to Baylor University in Waco where a large devastating tornado hit the entire area. Then during college, he worked in "Happy Patch" ranch in Brownwood, Texas in the flat dry lands beyond the Texas "hill country" to the west of Waco to pay bills. He rode the ranch pulling rattlesnakes out of holes. Here the familiar dairy cows of Wisconsin were substituted for the West Texas cattle of "Happy Patch."

The Korean War, academia at U. Texas, Fulbrights at the Frei Universitat Germany, and Universidad de Salamanca (Spain) and in Mexico followed by the University of Iowa writers' workshop intervened. But Andrew was drawn back to the boreal forests of northern Minnesota in his first teaching job at Bemidji State University, working with Native Americans. Then Andrew was called to St. Andrew's University of the "Great Books", where he lived at the edge of a Laurenberg, North Carolina forest. After several years, he joined the Peace Corps.

When Andrew left academia to arrive in Central East Africa as a member of the Peace Corps, he was mesmerized by the gigantic hills and the flat central high plains of Africa with abundant wildlife. The bears and wolves he loved had been exchanged for elephants and lions; the dairy cows exchanged were for wildebeest and water buffalo. His fascination with the African animals could only be expressed as "childlike." He felt totally at home in the hills of Africa, being posted first to Uganda during the Idi Amin uprising where he contracted a severe malarial infection (which finally killed him in 2013) and Tanzania, and then to Malawi for 3 years where he was Peace Corps Mission Director. He would drive across the plains in his Land Rover visiting the far-flung Peace Corps staff, while viewing the wildlife and vistas. Andrew would take all available times (never enough) to visit the "veld" in various parts of East Africa. So he became acquainted with South African, Malawi and Botswana and Burundi and the seacoast areas. He would also go on "breaks" to visit Madagascar on the coast or Egyptian ruins coming and going to the States. Later when he was the CEO of the not-for-profit non-governmental organization, Partnership for Productivity (PfP), he greatly enjoyed any opportunity to "get into the field" as part of PfP's work with the poorest of the poor throughout Africa. He could proudly point out that his organization from its inception in 1966 served village people by very, very small loan programs catering to these "poorest of the poor" throughout Africa from north (Egypt and Morocco) to South Africa and eventually to 68 nations in Africa, Asia, and Latin America/ Caribbean. So Andrew spent another 15 years and was given many opportunities to see African animals in the field. While CEO of Greater Caribbean and Asian Energy and Environment Foundation, there were electrical generating power plant assessments in Africa, African Ports environmentally assessed, newly found Gas and Oil fields and their accessory structure environmentally examined for the World Bank with many trips back and forth to East, North, and West Africa wherein more of Africa was explored in large adventures.

His final phase or "retirement from micro-enterprise" phase was spent in environmental healing of the earth after disasters and damage such as oil spills and earthquakes, with Andrew as CEO of the

Greater Caribbean and Asian Energy and Environment Foundation, where he helped correct the environmental placement of ports and national energy systems in places like Kenya, Equatorial Guinea, Cameroons in Africa, in Philippines, Thailand, Papua New Guinea in Asia, and Mexico, Haiti, Jamaica, and other Latin-American/Caribbean countries, and the Middle East's Arabian Gulf. Restoration of habitat vegetation along seacoasts throughout the tropical world was a large part of this task. In this final phase he traveled extensively while participating in mitigating for damages to sustain natural ecosystems while working with UN agencies and national governments. This work also took him to Egypt, Kenya, Tanzania, Guinea Bissau, Equatorial Guinea, Morocco, and areas along the Arabian Gulf, Red Sea and Indian Ocean, Philippines, Thailand, Burma, Papua New Guinea as well as many other global areas. At home in the USA, Andrew co-led some of the largest underwater restorations of submerged habitat in the world in the Gulf of Mexico (Texas) and Florida, and traveled the world teaching restoration for future marine sustainability.

All this time he wrote poetry about what he was seeing. He never took photographs because he said he remembered the experience in his mind and then transmitted to papers. There was always the poetry notebook in his hand into which he scribbled.

So never before in the many books and published poems has Andrew's environmental ethic, his insight, his intense attachment to nature, his comprehension of the ancient aspects of the earth and her living animals and plants been explicit. His multiple other poetry books and single poems seen at Andrewoerkepoetry.org hint at his strong attachment to a healthy earth. *Elephant Cake Walk* was one of the final manuscripts Andrew pored over, and worked on during his last weeks, with grandfatherly desire that his grandchildren Cashen and Odin would love the animals he wrote about.

(Several biographies available and list of poems and books at andrewoerkepoetry.org)

Cynthia Moss, et al., Photographs

We are most honored to have a woman who devoted her entire life and passion to saving and healing elephants in a most fragile and disappearing segment of East Africa collaborate in this work of art and in outreach to the many who cannot live a life of environmental healing. Cynthia Moss is the most effective advocate and voice for sustaining the African elephants in their habitat. Her life is devoted to bringing the ethics of living creatures "on the brink of disaster" to the attention of the global public, many of whom assist by donations to this effort. We are intensely grateful for the marvelous artistic quality of her photos in this book. Even Walt Disney staff could not have made the spirit of these magnificent animals more comprehensible to the reader.

Hopefully, the reader will enter the enchanted worlds of poet Andrew Oerke and photos of Cynthia Moss and others in reading this volume and wish to outreach to save the ecosystems and species on the brink of extinction in Africa and around the world. The readers can immerse themselves in this collaborative work of art, of tribute to Africa's environment.

For many fine photos go to on Cynthia's web site elephanttrust.org.

–Anitra Thorhaug Ph.D.

Biscayne Bay, Fl. at the intersection of the Everglades National Park and Florida Keys National Marine Sanctuary while today sitting in our hutte on Lake Superior, Wisconsin. August 2017.

Editor's Note:

This expanded edition of *Elephant Cakewalk* includes the beautiful photographs of **Carol Leadbetter**, a photographer of great talent whose commitment as a conservationist runs deep. Her haunting image of "ghost" elephants tells the story of a possible extinction of these blessed creatures. The images do not attempt to "illustrate" Oerke's poems, but rather give the reader a feeling for this remarkable continent. She describes her artistic mission, "*To capture through the camera the beauty of the landscapes and the cultures of the world. To display the essence of a scene or moment and invite the viewer to create their own interpretation of the image.*"

Leadbetter's work with mixed media include digital collage, encaustics, and transfers on alternative surfaces. Ms. Leadbetter prints all her own work using archival inks and papers. Her photographic interests include travel, portraiture, floral and human figure work. She lives in the Washington area and is represented by the Waverly Street Gallery, Bethesda, Maryland.

www.ingramcontent.com/pod-product-compliance
Ingram Content Group UK Ltd.
Pitfield, Milton Keynes, MK11 3LW, UK
UKHW062301290726
14090UKWH00017B/821

9 780997 262971